The ABCs of the UCC

of the

UCC

D1236005

Article 2A: Leases

Third Edition

Amelia H. Boss
Stephen T. Whelan

Uniform Commercial Code Committee

ABA Business Law Section
AMERICAN BAR ASSOCIATION

Cover design by ABA Publishing.

Page layout by Quadrum Solutions.

The materials contained herein represent the opinions of the authors and editors and should not be construed to be the views or opinions of the law firms or companies with whom such persons are in partnership with, associated with, or employed by, nor of the American Bar Association or the Business Law Section unless adopted pursuant to the bylaws of the Association.

Nothing contained in this book is to be considered as the rendering of legal advice for specific cases, and readers are responsible for obtaining such advice from their own legal counsel. This book and any forms and agreements herein are intended for educational and informational purposes only.

Printed in the United States of America.

17 16 15 14 13 5 4 3 2 1

Library of Congress Cataloging-in-Publication Data

Boss, Amelia H., and Stephen T. Whelan, authors.

ABCs of the UCC : Article 2A, Leases / by Amy Boss, Steve Whelan, and the UCC Committee, Business Law Section, American Bar Association. —3rd edition.

    pages cm

Includes bibliographical references.

ISBN 978-1-62722-393-5 (alk. paper)

1. Leases—United States—States. 2. Personal property—United States—States. 3. Uniform commercial code. Leases. I. American Bar Association. UCC Committee, author. II. American Bar Association. Business Law Section, sponsoring body. III. Title. IV. Title: Article 2A, Leases. V. Title: Leases.

KF946B668 2013

346.7304'346—dc23

                2013043671

Discounts are available for books ordered in bulk. Special consideration is given to state bars, CLE programs, and other bar related organizations. Inquire at Book Publishing, ABA Publishing, American Bar Association, 321 N. Clark Street, Chicago, Illinois 60654-7598.

www.ShopABA.org

CONTENTS

Chapter 5

Chapter 6

Chapter 7

Chapter 8

FOREWORD

Since it was first proposed over seventy years ago, the Uniform Commercial Code has become both an indispensable part of the study of law and an essential part of legal practice. Adopted by all fifty states, the Code has been hailed as one of the great products of American law. Its impact is by no means limited to the United States. The Code has become an important U.S. export: other nations have modeled their laws after our Uniform Commercial Code, and portions of the Code and its principles have been carried over into international instruments such as the United Nations Convention on the International Sale of Goods, the United Nations Convention on the Assignment of Receivables in International Trade, and the International Institute for the Unification of Private Law (UNIDROIT) Convention on International Interests in Mobile Equipment.

Despite the importance and impact of the Code, many practitioners and students find it difficult to master. Its provisions, followed by official comments, cross-references, and notes, often seem impenetrable. The problem stems from several sources.

First, as Grant Gilmore, one of the principal drafters of the Code, once observed, the Code sometimes appears to have been written in its own shorthand. The keys to deciphering that shorthand are frequently found in the definitions to the Code and are often found in an understanding of non-Code law.

Second, no single provision of the Code can truly be understood without an understanding of the other provisions of the Code and its overarching purposes, policies, and concepts. The interconnectedness of the Code's provisions and the importance of its often unarticulated policies require extended study for mastery.

Third, the Code, even on its own terms, does not purport to contain all the law there is on a particular subject; the Code may be uniform, but it is not comprehensive. The Code invites us to consult non-Code law to "fill in the gaps" in its coverage.

Last, the Uniform Commercial Code itself is not "law." Rather, the Code is adopted on a state-by-state basis; individual states may make nonuniform amendments during the adoption process, or state courts may interpret its provisions in a nonuniform manner, making it all the more difficult for the new practitioner or student to master.

This series of books, *The ABCs of the UCC*, a project of the Uniform Commercial Code Committee of the American Bar Association's Section of Business Law, has been making the Code accessible to practitioner and student alike for almost fifteen years. Free of the footnotes and the extensive convoluted discussions that often accompany legal literature, each book is written to present the basic concepts and operation of the Code articles in a simple, straightforward manner. No attempt is made to treat the Code in an in-depth manner, nor to cite to all possibly relevant authorities and cases. Rather, the goal is to provide the reader with the framework and basic knowledge of the Code necessary to orient the reader for future work or research. Thus, this series of books does not supplant, but rather complements, more intensive treatments of the subjects.

Each book in the series is devoted to one of the articles of the Code, yet they are intended to form a coherent whole which, taken together, provides an overview of the Code in operation. Each book is written by a distinguished person in the field of commercial law whom colleagues consider an expert in the field. The focus is on the uniform text of the Code: the text as adopted by the sponsors of the Code, the American Law Institute and the National Conference of Commissioners on Uniform State Laws. While the focus is on the uniform version, each book, where appropriate, points out important nonuniform amendments and divergent judicial treatment of the Code provisions.

In 1965, Grant Gilmore warned that the enactment of the Code and of Article 9 did not mark the end of the process of change and development in the field of commercial law. His comments were more perceptive than he could have realized. Since his prescient words were penned, the Code has undergone extensive revision and change: new articles were added, others replaced or amended, and one has even been repealed. The well-advised practitioner and student realize that the process of learning should be an ongoing one; the knowledge gained from their reading of this current series of ready reference books should nonetheless provide a firm foundation for supplementation in the future.

The Uniform Commercial Code Committee of the ABA's Section of Business Law welcomes the opportunity to provide these tools to the legal profession. We hope that you find this series of books useful for your needs.

Amelia H. Boss
Drexel University Earle Mack School of Law
Editor

PREFACE

Leases of goods have existed for centuries, but until Article 2A was added to the Uniform Commercial Code in 1987, there was no coherent body of law to assist practitioners and judges in interpreting these contracts. The beauty of Article 2A is that, with a few exceptions, it leaves the parties the freedom to write their lease agreement as they wish. The difficulty a leasing practitioner might have with Article 2A is that it borrows heavily from several sources—such as Article 2 on sales and Article 9 on secured transactions—which people may not necessarily associate with a common law bailment transaction. Seventeen years after Article 2A was first adopted, there is a large population that still does not understand how this article works. Indeed, many practitioners are unaware of this major addition to the Code and how it affects transactions such as leases of aircraft or other categories of capital equipment.

That is why this book was written. Attorneys for lessors and lessees, as well as third parties such as lenders and equipment suppliers who are involved with lease transactions, need a concise, readable introduction to Article 2A. In particular, because Article 2A has contributed mightily to clarifying the law regarding rights of third parties, events of default, and remedies, the authors have devoted significant space to explaining these portions of Article 2A. This volume should be especially helpful for a practitioner faced with his or her first leasing transaction. Because of space limitations, this book does not discuss any nonuniform provisions that may have been enacted in some states.

Since the first edition of this book was published in 1997, the Code has undergone extensive revisions. Revisions to Article 1 (2002), Article 2 (2003) and Article 9 (1999) have required conforming amendments to Article 2A, although as will be discussed, the 2003 amendments to Article 2A were subsequently withdrawn.

In addition, an established and growing body of judicial precedent interpreting and applying Article 2A is now available. This short book will, we hope, serve as a guide to all these developments.

The authors would like to thank the Business Law Section of the American Bar Association for their continued commitment to producing timely, useful publications for the practicing lawyer. We would also like to thank Lauren Strebel, Earle Mack School of Law class of 2014, and Ramesh Dhanaraj, associate attorney with Blank Rome LLP, for their assistance on this edition.

Stephen T. Whelan
Amelia H. Boss
September 2013

CHAPTER

1

INTRODUCTION

A. History of Article 2A

Examples of leasing transactions can be traced back to Roman times, but it has only been within recent years, since the original enactment of the Uniform Commercial Code (UCC or Code), that leasing as an industry has grown and flourished. Fed by such benefits as favorable tax and accounting treatment, leasing began to grow tremendously during the 1950s and 1960s, soon coming into its own as a distinct industry.

Despite its ancient origins, the law applicable to leasing transactions was far from clear. Efforts were made to draw principles from the ancient law of bailments; sales law was often used by analogy; and the law of conditional sales, secured transactions, licensing, and real estate leasing law were frequently invoked. The uncertain nature of the law of leasing led, in the early 1980s, to efforts to codify the law of leasing. Although originally proposed and formulated as a "free-standing," independent, and uniform law, when this new codification finally emerged in 1987 it was presented as the first new addition to the UCC, Article 2A on leases.

The choice of the article number was a reflection of the fact that this new body of leasing law was based primarily on the sales law found in Article 2 of the Code. Oklahoma, in 1988, was the first state to enact Article 2A, followed by South Dakota, California, and several other states. From the very beginning, however, Article 2A was subjected to nonuniform amendments which undercut its status as a "uniform law." Academic critique began, and several states, including New York and California, raised serious questions about specific provisions of Article 2A. As a result of these criticisms, questions, and other input, Official Amendments to Article 2A were proposed and adopted in 1990, leading to the "1990 Official Text."

Subsequently, however, efforts began to revise both the sales and leasing articles of the Code; these culminated in 2003 with the final adoption of the 2003 Amendments to Articles 2 and 2A. Although the amendments were much more limited in scope than had been originally anticipated when the revision process began, they failed to achieve any enactments by state legislatures, with the result that in 2011 the sponsors of the UCC (the American Law Institute and the Uniform Law Commission) withdrew them from the Official Text. Consequently, this edition focuses on the 1990 Official Text of Article 2A rather than the 2003 Amendments. Article 2A has been adopted in 51 jurisdictions (but not Louisiana or Puerto Rico). Additionally, Article 1, which applies to all transactions covered by the UCC, including leases under Article 2A, was revised (and renumbered) in 2001; as of September 2013 revised Article 1 has been adopted by all states (with the exception of Georgia, Missouri, New York, South Carolina, and Wyoming), the District of Columbia, and the Virgin Islands (but not Puerto Rico). All citations to Article 1 that follow are to the 2001 revisions with the prerevision citation following in brackets.

B. Basic Principles and Interpretation of Article 2A

One of the basic tenets on which the entire UCC is based is the notion that the parties to a transaction should be able to agree to the rules applicable to them, and set forth those terms under which they intend to do business. § 1-302(a) [§ 1-102(3)]. This concept of freedom of contract runs throughout Article 2A. § 2A-101, Official Comment. The latitude extended to lessors and lessees includes the ability to contractually alter the obligations imposed on them by Article 2A. *Id.* The only limitation is that the obligations of good faith, diligence, reasonableness, and care imposed by the Code may not be disclaimed, although the parties may set forth the standards by which such obligations are to be measured. § 1-302(b) [§ 1-102(3)]. Thus, in many fully negotiated lease deals, Article 2A will function as a backdrop against which the terms of the transaction are negotiated. In nonnegotiated deals, or where the agreement entered into by the parties is found unenforceable, the Code provides a comprehensive set of rules governing the transaction and providing its terms.

There are, of course, limitations on the parties' ability to agree. For example, in *Danka Funding Co. v. Sky City Casino*, 747 A.2d 837 (N.J. Super. Ct. Law Div. 1999), the court upheld an Indian Tribe's sovereign immunity from civil suit despite the existence of a forum selection clause in an equipment lease. Furthermore, as discussed below, a court has the ability to refuse to enforce the lease agreement, or any part of it, should it find the agreement or its terms to be unconscionable. § 2A-108(1). The obligation of good faith in the performance or enforcement of any lease contract is likewise imposed by the Code via Article 1 and is not disclaimable. §§ 1-304, 1-302(b) [§§ 1-203, 1-102(3), 2A-103(1)(m)]. Moreover, as will be discussed below, in the case of consumer leases, the consumer receives special protection that may override the terms of the lease agreement.

Article 2A is, nonetheless, based on a model of freedom of contract, and contains relatively few mandatory provisions. There is no general requirement that a lessor file a financing statement or similar document to protect its interest in the leased goods. Nonetheless, lessors should proceed cautiously. First, prudent lessors will continue to file protective financing statements under § 9-505, thereby guarding against the possibility that the lease will be found, not to create a "lease," but to create a security interest under §§ 1-201(35) (defining a security interest) and 1-203 [§ 1-201(37)] (distinguishing between a security interest and a lease), potentially leading to the defeat of the lessor's interest under the rules found in Article 9. Second, where the lessor anticipates that the leased goods will become attached to real estate, the lessor should make a fixture filing. § 2A-309. Last, certificate of title statutes in many jurisdictions may require that lessors note their interest in such items as automobiles, trailers, mobile homes, boats, and farm tractors on the certificate of title covering the leased item in order to assert those interests against third parties. § 2A-104.

Leasing law found in Article 2A continues to be supplemented by other law, such as the law of estoppel, fraud, and mistake. § 1-103(b) [§ 1-103]. In addition, an applicable rule of law that establishes a different rule for consumers will continue to apply and will not be preempted by Article 2A's provisions. § 2A-104. Thus, in *B & S Marketing Enterprises, LLC v. Consumer Protection Division*, 153 Md. App. 130, 835 A.2d 215 (Md. Ct. Spec. App. 2003), the court applied Maryland Consumer Loan Law rather than the UCC in determining whether a purported sale-leaseback was in reality a loan that violated usury laws. Similarly, in *LaChapelle v. Toyota Motor Credit Corp.,* 102 Cal.App.4th 977, 126 Cal.Rptr.2d 32 (Cal. Ct. App. 2002), a controversy involving whether truth-in-lending wording was required in the contract, the court noted that although it concluded that the outcome of the case would be the same under California's Article 2A or under California's Vehicle Leasing Act or Consumer Legal Remedies Act, in the event of a conflict, Article 2A would give way to the consumer law.

As Article 2A is a relatively recent "addition" to the UCC, courts will undoubtedly be called upon to interpret its provisions in cases of first impression. These courts will not, however, be writing on a completely clean slate. To the extent that Article 2A's provisions are based upon comparable provisions of Article 2 on sales, with only minor changes to reflect changes in leasing terminology, decisions under Article 2 should be "viewed as persuasive but not binding" in determining the meaning of parallel Article 2A provisions. § 2A-101, Official Comment. Similarly, the Official Comments to the sales provisions may be of guidance in interpreting the parallel leasing provisions. In instances where the leasing provision is drawn from Article 9 on secured transactions, as is the case with respect to the right to repossession, it is reasonable to expect that the decisions under the Article 9 counterpart section on such issues as what constitutes breach of the peace will be relevant.

Care should be taken, however, to distinguish those situations where the drafters of Article 2A affirmatively rejected Article 2's provisions as a model. Where legitimate differences between the articles exist, blind adherence to "parallelism" would be unwarranted. As a noted commentator has remarked, "Leasing is distinctive."

CHAPTER

2

Applicability

A. Article 2A Affects Only "True" Leases

According to its terms, Article 2A "applies to any transaction, regardless of form, that creates a lease." § 2A-102. Even though § 2A-103(a)(p) [§ 2A-103(1)(j)] defines a "lease" as "a transfer of the right to possession and use of goods for a period [term] in return for consideration," the section further states that the creation of a security interest is not a lease. The crucial provision thus becomes the detailed definition of "security interest" in §§ 1-201(35) along with § 1-203 [§ 1-201(37)], which enables the practitioner to distinguish between a true lease (governed by Article 2A) and a security interest, also referred to as a lease "intended to create a security interest" (governed by Article 9). Article 2A, incorporating the provisions of §§ 1-201(35) and 1-203 of Revised Article 1 (or § 1-201(37) of prerevision Article 1), relies upon objective criteria rather than indicia of intent in order to make the distinction. Thus, the court in *In re HomePlace Stores, Inc.*, 228 B.R. 88 (Bankr. D. Del. 1998) held that the intent of the parties, regardless of how explicit, could not control the determination of the agreement's "true lease" status.

The terms that the parties use to describe the transaction are not determinative of whether the lease is either a "true" lease or a "lease intended for security." Instead, the substance and the structure of the transaction control. In *B & S Marketing Enterprises, LLC v. Consumer Protection Division*, 153 Md. App. 130, 835 A.2d 215 (Md. Ct. Spec. App. 2003), the court held that under Article 2A as well as state consumer laws, a purported "sale-leaseback" was nothing more than a loan where the "lessor" made efforts not to inform customers of their option to return the property "leased" and instead emphasized repurchasing the items as the only way to end the "lease." The court also found it significant that the items "sold" and "leased back" to the customer had little or no value to the "lessor," the "lessor" had no expectation of any meaningful residual interest in the property, the "lessor" never demanded the return of the property when the customer defaulted on "rental payments," and the "sale" amount was constant regardless of the type or condition of the item "sold."

Nevertheless, some courts continue to look at the form of the transaction; e.g., *NationsBank of North Carolina, N.A. v. Capital Associates International, Inc.*, 916 F. Supp. 549 (W.D.N.C. 1996), where the court cited statements in the contract that it was a "true lease" and an "agreement of lease only" to support its conclusion that the contract was a true lease.

In common understanding, a lease is a transaction where the lessor retains some interest in the goods (known as its residual interest); upon completion of the lease term, possession and use of the goods revert to the lessor. In contrast, in a secured transaction, upon satisfactory completion of the transaction (i.e., payment of the underlying loan) the secured party has no further interest in the goods; rather the lessee/debtor has full possession and ownership of the goods. Thus, in differentiating between leases and security interests, there are two main tests: (a) the nature of the lessee's obligation to pay; and (b) the interest, if any, retained by the lessor.

First, if the lessee has the right to terminate the lease at any time and hence to end its obligation to pay, the transaction can be nothing other than a true lease. There is no expectation in such an instance that absent breach, the lessee/debtor will retain possession and ownership of the goods. On this basis, courts have regularly ruled that so called terminable "rent-to-own" contracts are true leases. In *In re Jarrells*, 205 B.R. 994 (Bankr. M.D. Ga. 1997), *In re Yarbrough*, 211 B.R. 654 (Bankr. W.D. Tenn. 1997) and *In re Street*, 214 B.R. 779 (Bankr. W.D. Pa. 1997), the respective courts noted the lessees' ability to terminate the contract by ending the monthly "rental" payments without making any additional payments upon termination in ruling that the contracts were true leases.

The analysis is less evident if the lessee can terminate the lease only upon payment of a lump sum termination value. Although the definition of "security interest" and the accompanying comments provide no direct guidance in this respect, the issue is somewhat easier to resolve if the question is phrased as whether the lessor has any meaningful expectation of reacquiring the goods. If the right to terminate requires payment of only a nominal sum, then it would be conceivable that the lessee might choose to exercise the option to avoid its more substantial payment obligations under the lease. Thus, the existence of the right to terminate upon payment of a nominal sum, like the unlimited right to terminate, demonstrates that it is likely that the goods will be returned to the lessor, hence that the lessor has a reasonable expectation of a residual interest in the goods, and therefore, that the lease is a true lease.

On the other hand, if the right to terminate requires payment of a substantial sum of money, e.g., an amount equal to or greater than the present value of the rents owed for the remainder of the lease, it is unlikely that a reasonable lessee will choose to exercise that termination right. The termination payment effectively operates as a penalty, forcing the reasonable lessee to continue performing under the lease. Additionally, the existence of a bargain purchase option may provide the lessor with little expectation of receiving the goods and capturing their residual value. Thus, the existence of the termination right itself should not dictate true lease status; the lease could well amount to a "secured transaction" if other elements of a security interest (such as a high termination value and a bargain purchase option) are present.

Assuming the lessee has no right to terminate (or may terminate only upon payment of a substantial price), the lease is not automatically a true lease. Instead, a second step in the analysis requires examination of the other terms of the lease to determine whether the lessor nonetheless has a reasonable expectation that upon termination of the lease term it will reacquire use and possession of the goods to a meaningful extent. In making that determination, key lease provisions to consider are (i) the term of the lease; (ii) the presence of options to renew; and (iii) the presence of options to buy. Note, however, that the presence of a right to terminate under the first step may preclude a finding that the transaction is a sale under the second step. See *In re Copeland*, 238 B.R. 801, 805-806 (Bankr. E.D. Ark. 1999) (lease included a right to purchase the equipment at the end of the lease for $1 but, because of a right to terminate, nonetheless was deemed a "true lease.").

The essence of the second test is whether the lessor has an expectation of reacquiring a meaningful residual in the goods upon termination of the lease. See *In re Murray*, 191 B.R. 309, 315 (E.D. Pa. 1996), aff'd 201 B.R. 381 (E.D. Pa. 1996) ("key emphasis... is on whether [the lessor] retains a meaningful residual interest in the [leased equipment]."); *Ray Lebron d/b/a Lebron Electronics v. Citicorp Vendor Finance, Inc.*, 2004 WL 1615837 (Tex. Ct. App. 2004) (recharacterization where both steps indicated transaction was a lease.) The lessor's expectation may be undercut by a provision in the lease whereby the lessee has (a) either the obligation or the option to acquire the goods for their "remaining economic life" (which life is determined "at the time the transaction is entered into") or (b) either a purchase or renewal option at less than fair market value. § 1-203(b) [§ 1-201(37)(a)]. A lease containing such a provision probably is a "lease intended for security." This second test can be measured in four ways.

The lease is for the full economic life of the goods. If the lease extends to the end of the economic life of the goods, upon the completion of the lease term, the goods will be valueless; thus, the lessor's expectation of the residual is meaningless. For example, suppose there is a lease of a $15,000 car that begins in 2004. A "Bluebook" lists the estimated economic life of that car's make and model. Assume further that the "Bluebook" lists the car's useful economic value as $2,000 in 2008 and $0 in 2012. If the lease terminates in 2008, the lessor regains $2,000 of "useful economic life" in the goods, and the lease is a true lease, since the anticipated residual value at that time is greater than a nominal amount. However, if the lease lasts through 2012, the lessor will never regain any useful economic value in the leased goods upon expiration of the lease term, and the lease is a lease "intended for security." Leases intended for security are disguised security interests that fall under the scope of Article 9 rather than Article 2A. See *In re Fleming Companies, Inc.*, 308 B.R. 693 (Bankr. D. Del. 2004) (lease held in substance a security agreement, where goods would have little or no value at end of lease term). But in *TFG-Illinois, LP v. United Maintenance Co.*, 2011 WL 5239728 (D. Utah 2011), the court found that, even if the equipment had no value to third parties, it still had some remaining economic life insofar as it retained "in place" value to a lessee in possession. And *In re Gateway Ethanol, LLC*, 415 B.R. 486 (Bankr. D. Kan. 2009) correctly concluded that the lease was not for the entire remaining economic life of the goods, where the lease term was five years and the anticipated useful life at lease inception was fifteen to twenty years. The decision also correctly observed that the equipment was not unique to the lessee and hence would have economic value to another user after expiration of the lease term.

The lessee is bound to renew for the remaining full economic life of the goods, or is bound to become the owner of the goods. Suppose that, in the example above, the lease was drafted to terminate in 2008 but that the lessee was nonetheless obligated to renew for a second four-year term. Courts correctly view such situations as forcing the lessee to lease the goods for the entire economic life of the goods, with no meaningful residual value left for the lessor, and deem such transactions to be leases intended for security. Similarly, if the lease obliged the lessee to buy the rented goods, the lessor would never regain any useful economic life of the goods, and the lease would be a disguised security interest.

The lessee has an option to renew for the economic life of the goods for "nominal" or no additional consideration. Here again, the important element is whether the lessor has any reasonable expectation of recovering any economic life of the leased goods. Article 2A makes two presumptions in the event that the lessee can renew the lease by paying little or no additional consideration. The first presumption is that the lessor asks for little or no additional consideration only in circumstances where the lessee already has paid for the entire useful economic life of the goods during the earlier term. Article 2A next presumes that the lessee will act rationally and exercise the renewal option, so that it can retain the remaining economic life for which it already paid. In any event, the lessor's expectation of getting the goods back is no longer meaningful so the lease is deemed a disguised security interest.

The lessee's rational choices may be affected by external circumstances e.g., the costs it may incur for failing to renew or purchase. *In re Kentuckiana Medical Center, LLC*, 455 B.R. 694 (Bankr. S.D. Ind. 2011) noted that if the lessee did not exercise its purchase option, it had to make up any shortfall in the lessor's cost of the equipment and the purchase option price. Because the reasonably predictable cost of returning the equipment thus exceeded the purchase option price, the court ruled that the lessee was compelled to exercise the purchase option and hence that the contract was a security device rather than a true lease.

In re Ecco Drilling Co., Ltd., 390 B. R. 221 (Bankr. E.D. Tex. 2008) involved leased drilling rigs which were so essential to the lessee's business that the lessee effectively was compelled to exercise the purchase option. Further supporting this conclusion was the option price, which was the greater of 15 percent of the value at lease inception or 60 percent of the going concern value of the lessee. *In re Pillowtex*, 349 F.3d 711 (3d Cir. 2003) held the contract to be a security arrangement, even though it was not a secured financing under any of the Section 1-201(37) tests, where the lessee had several end-of-term options such that it could "effectively compel [the lessor] to abandon the [leased equipment] to avoid the exorbitant expense of acquiring and installing replacement" equipment, thereby depriving the lessor of any meaningful residual value in the goods.

The lessee has an option to purchase for "nominal" or no additional consideration. This situation is analogous to the prior example, and Article 2A makes the same two presumptions. If the lessor will allow the lessee to own the goods for little or no additional payment, then either the rational lessee has already paid for the useful economic life of the goods and will claim ownership, or the useful economic life of the goods has expired. Since any economically rational lessee will therefore exercise the option, the lessor will not regain any remaining economic life of the leased goods and the lease is a disguised security interest. For instance, in the vehicle example above, if the lease granted the lessee the option to buy the goods in 2008 for $500, such a bargain purchase option is likely to be exercised, and it is unlikely that the lessor would realize the full remaining economic life of the leased goods. By contrast, in *In re Rebel Rents*, 291 B.R. 520 (Bankr. C.D. Cal. 2003), the court found a true lease where the lessee failed to meet its burden of proof that the contracts contained a nominal purchase option or left the lessor with no meaningful residual value in the vehicles. § 1-203(b) (1)-(4) [§ 1-201(37)(a)-(d)].

If the lease meets any of the four criteria discussed above and also lacks a "right to terminate" as discussed earlier, then it fails to qualify as a "true lease." It will be deemed to be a disguised security interest, and Article 2A will not apply. Thus, the court in *In re Super Feeders*, 236 B.R. 267 (Bankr. D. Neb. 1999) ruled that a lease which gave the lessee a nominal fixed price purchase option (valued at 20 percent of the fair market value) at the end of the lease term was a disguised security interest. Similarly, a "side agreement" containing a purchase option of $1 was considered part of the lease in *In re Kim*, 232 B.R. 324 (Bankr. E.D. Pa. 1999), and destroyed "true lease" status.

Occasionally, courts have failed to analyze critically the nature of such options. One such example is *In re Lykes Bros. Steamship Co.*, 196 B.R. 574 (Bankr. M.D. Fla. 1996). There, the court ruled that an early buyout option permitting the lessee to buy the vessels five years prior to the expiration date of the lease for the greater of $44 million or fair market value made the contract a disguised security interest. The court reasoned that the lessee would be economically compelled to buy the vessels because the remaining lease payments of $91 million were so much greater than the buyout price. However, the court failed to notice that the fair market value could have exceeded $44 million, thereby undermining the economic compulsion argument. In another decision, *Caterpillar Financial Services Corp. v. Wells*, 651 A.2d 507 (N.J. Super. Ct. Law Div. 1994), the court correctly ruled that a bargain purchase option at lease-end which would almost certainly be exercised converted the "lease" into a security interest, but incorrectly cited irrelevant factors such as lessor's filing of a financing statement.

Questions will undoubtedly arise as to what constitutes "nominal consideration" for either a purchase or renewal option. Again, the focus is on whether the option price is so low that the lessee has no economic reason not to acquire ownership, and consequently that the lessor has no reasonable expectation of reacquiring the goods.

Section 1-203(d) [1-201(37)] gives three illustrations which assist in determining what constitutes "nominal" consideration. First, if the renewal option price is stated to be the fair market price for the use of the goods for the renewal period, then by definition the option is not nominal. This is not a situation where any economically rational lessee would automatically exercise the renewal option, so that the lessor retains a reasonable expectation that (until the options are exercised) it will get the goods back upon termination of the lease. Second, if the purchase option is the fair market value of the goods at the time of the exercise of the option, then the price is not nominal; it is not preordained that an economically rational lessee would exercise the option. The third illustration would apply in instances where the purchase option is to be exercised not at the end of the lease, but prior to the lease's expiration. In that case, if the purchase option is sufficiently "less than the lessee's reasonably predictable cost of performing" under the remainder of the lease without exercise of this mid-term purchase option such that any rational lessee would exercise that option, then the price is deemed nominal. If an economically rational lessee must pay $100 per month for the remaining twenty-four months of the lease, but has the option of purchasing the goods today for only $600, it will choose to exercise the purchase option and not continue leasing the goods.

A particular kind of lease, mostly used for vehicle leases where the lessee is in the position to control how much wear and tear the leased property receives, and hence whether the lessor will receive its projected residual value at lease expiration, is called a "TRAC lease" (for Terminal Rent Adjustment Clause). A TRAC lease will require the vehicle to be appraised at lease expiration; the lessee must pay the lessor any shortfall below the projected residual value, and the lessor must pay the lessee any excess of the appraised value above the projected value. As of early 2013, 48 states and the District of Columbia had adopted statutes declaring that the mere inclusion of such a clause would not cause the contract to be deemed as creating a security interest. See *In re Double G Trucking of ArkLatex*, 432 B.R. 789 (Bankr. W.D. Ark. 2010).

In *In re HB Logistics, LLC*, 460 B.R. 291 (Bankr. N.D. Ala. 2011), the court observed that such reallocation of the risk as to the projected residual value is not equivalent to transferring all risk of ownership of the leased goods. Such a clause arguably functions to assure that the lessor does indeed retain the benefit of its bargained-for residual interest, in the event that the lessee's use of the vehicle impairs the lessor's residual interest. Conversely, if the lessee's use increases the anticipated value of the residual interest, the lessee has bestowed a benefit on the lessor and deserves to be compensated under the TRAC provision. But in *In re Lash*, 2010 WL 514170 (Bankr. M.D.N.C. 2010), the court failed to apply the Utah TRAC statute, instead choosing to use the traditional economic analysis to conclude that the TRAC provision removed any meaningful residual interest from the lessor. The decision is even more remarkable because the Utah statute goes beyond the TRAC laws in other states and provides that a TRAC clause "does not create a sale or security interest." Utah Code Ann. Section 41-1a-609(2)(2003).

It is important to be able to determine at the time of contracting whether an agreement is a true lease or a disguised security interest. For that very reason, the Code provides that in determining whether something is "reasonably predictable" or in determining the "remaining economic life of the goods," the key is the facts and circumstances at the time the transaction is entered into. § 1-201(b)(35) [§ 1-201(37)]. Assume, for example, that when the parties enter into a ten-year lease of a piece of equipment, they understand at the time of the transaction that the equipment has an economic life of twenty years. Under these circumstances, the lease would be a true lease even though later changes in technology make the equipment obsolete (and therefore without any remaining economic life) before the end of the ten-year term. Similarly, although the Code does not address the situation directly, if at the time the lease transaction is entered into the parties fix a purchase option price of $8,000 for the goods, a figure that represents what the parties believed—at the time the transaction was entered into, in good faith, and in accordance with reasonable commercial standards—the goods would be worth when the option would be exercised, the purchase option should be considered "nonnominal" even though later market changes substantially increase the market value of the goods. Moreover, the anticipated residual value of the equipment at the end of the lease term must be considered in calculating whether the early buyout option price is nominal.

But in *In re QDS Components, Inc.*, 292 B.R. 313 (Bankr. S.D. Ohio 2002), the court noted that the combination of "net" lease obligations, a fixed price purchase option, and an early termination provision (by paying the discounted present value of the remaining rents plus the option purchase price), did not destroy true lease status, where the purchase option price was not nominal compared to the residual value as estimated at the time of the lease's inception rather than subsequently at the time of the lessee's default.

Even if the agreement does not contain any of the four criteria listed for the second test, it may nonetheless still be a disguised security interest rather than a true lease, depending upon the facts of each case. In making that determination, however, there are some criteria that the Code cautions are not sufficient in and of themselves to mandate the finding of a security interest. These criteria, listed in § 1-203(b) [the third paragraph of § 1-201(37)], are:

- whether the present value of the consideration paid by the lessee is equal to or greater than the fair market value of the goods;
- whether the lessee bears certain indicia of ownership, such as the risk of loss or duty to pay taxes, insurance, filing fees, or maintenance; or
- whether the lessee merely has an option to renew the lease or buy the goods, unless the options fall under the tests mentioned above.

These factors are ones to which courts have looked in the past, but generally they are contract clauses which can be found in both secured transactions and leases. Frequently, lessors will lease an item at a rental equal to or greater than the present value of the purchase price of the item; yet the lessor will be expecting to reacquire the item upon termination of the lease term, often calculating its profit by reference to the value of the item upon termination. Thus, these "full pay-out" clauses may be found in true leases and are not determinative of security lease status. Instead, the pertinent inquiry is whether the lessor will reacquire the goods while they have any remaining economic life.

Similarly, lessees frequently agree to pay taxes, maintenance fees, and the like. The presence of such terms in the lease should not be used by themselves to recharacterize the lease as creating a security interest, since such obligations usually represent a trade-off, with the lessee paying less fixed rent in exchange for assuming such costs. However, despite the explicit caveat of § 1-201(37), some courts will nevertheless deem purported leases to be security arrangements based solely on such criteria. See *Bantera Bank v. Subway Equipment Leasing (In re Taylor)*, 209 B.R. 482 (Bankr. S.D. Ill. 1997).

B. Article 2A Applies Only to Leases of Goods

By its terms, Article 2A is applicable only to contracts for the "transfer of the right to possession and use of goods." "Goods" are defined as "all things that are movable at the time of identification to the lease contract, § 2A-103(1)(n) [§ 2A-103(1)(h)] or are fixtures. § 2A-309. This definition is drawn directly from Article 2, so the case law interpreting the term in the context of sales should be persuasive in the case of leases. Article 9 suggests that "goods" fall into four categories: "consumer goods," "equipment," "farm products," and "inventory." § 9-102(a)(23), (33), (34), (48). A major unresolved area is the application of Article 2A (or Article 2) to transfers of information such as software; while these transfers may be accompanied by the transfer of a tangible item such as a CD or a car, software may also be downloaded. Whether these are "goods" for purposes of the application of Article 2 or Article 2A remains uncertain.

C. Which State's Version of Article 2A Applies?

Although all jurisdictions (except Louisiana and Puerto Rico) have adopted the current version of Article 2A, resolution of leasing disputes may turn on which state's law applies to the lease contract. Under the general Code choice-of-law rules of Article 1, when a transaction bears a reasonable relation to this state and also to another state or nation the parties may chose the law to govern their rights and duties. In the absence of such an agreement, Article 2A would apply to transactions bearing an appropriate relation to the forum state. Thus, in *Information Leasing Corp. v. King*, 800 N.E.2d 73 (Ohio Ct. App. 2003), the court upheld a forum selection clause in a finance lease, stating that, "absent evidence of fraud or overreaching, a forum-selection clause contained in a commercial contract between business entities is valid and enforceable unless it can be clearly shown that the enforcement of the clause would be unreasonable or unjust." The law chosen by the parties must not violate the fundamental public policy of the state whose law would otherwise govern. See *Andin Int'l Inc. v. Matrix Funding Corp.* 194 Misc.2d 719 (N.Y. Sup. Ct. 2003).

There are additional limitations on choice-of-law clauses in consumer leases under Article 2A: the parties may not choose the law of a state unless either the consumer lessee resides there or the goods are to be used there. § 2A-106(1). The consumer lessee easily knows these states, and there is a strong policy basis for using those states' laws. In the business context, some states have non-Code statutes permitting choice of that state's law, even if the contract does not bear a reasonable relation thereto. *Cf.* N.Y. Gen. Oblig. Law § 5-1401 (McKinney 1989 and West Supp. 1997) (applying to any contract involving $250,000 or more). New Jersey law, however, cautions that the choice of law clause must be "conspicuous," just as a disclaimer of warranties clause must be, and that this applies even in a commercial lease if it is a contract of adhesion. *Fairfield Leasing Corp. v. Techni-Graphics, Inc.*, 607 A.2d 703 (N.J. Super. 1992).

CHAPTER

3

SPECIAL TYPES OF LEASES

The basic provisions of Article 2A are based on a paradigm of a two-party lease transaction negotiated at arm's-length between two parties of equal bargaining status. There are, however, two extremely important categories of leases that do not fit within this paradigm. First, there is the consumer lease, where the ability to bargain at arms-length is more theoretical than actual. As a result, special consumer rules were added in several places to give needed protection to consumer lessees.

Second, in the leasing industry, a form of transaction has developed in which the lessor merely serves as a financing party rather than as a typical dealer in the goods. The potential lessee chooses the item it wishes to acquire from a particular supplier, and (often through competitive bidding) selects a lessor who simultaneously purchases the goods from the supplier and leases them to the lessee. This tripartite transaction, called a finance lease under Article 2A, is also governed by special rules which recognize the financing role of the lessor and the unique relationship among the three parties.

A. Consumer Leases

Section 2A-103(1)(e) has created the concept of a "consumer lease" which arises when the lease is between (i) a lessor regularly engaged in the business of leasing or selling, and (ii) an individual who takes under the lease for a personal, family, or household purpose. A classic example of a consumer lessee would be the family that opts to lease its new family vehicle, or (on a shorter term) lease a rental car for a two-week vacation. As noted above, in this type of a lease there is seldom any bargaining on the part of the consumer lessee. Optional language in § 2A-103(e) allows a legislature to insert a dollar cap on leases designated as consumer leases; to date thirty jurisdictions have set such a cap in varying amounts ranging from $25,000 to $100,000.

Article 2A contains provisions unique to consumer leases. One consumer concern is the "at will" or insecurity clause in a lease agreement, which allows the lessor to accelerate all rentals due under the lease if it deems itself "insecure." Under such a clause, a lessee who believes its obligation is to pay $100 per month over the coming thirty-six months may find that the lessor has accelerated the rents and now demands a grand total of $3,600. Under § 2A-109, a lessor under a consumer lease who accelerates payments "at will" or because of insecurity has the burden of establishing its good faith in exercising that option. Although the party objecting to such acceleration has this burden in nonconsumer lease transactions, this section recognizes that the consumer lessee seldom has the resources to carry that burden, even if the requisite facts existed.

A second common concern with consumer leases, albeit a concern of the lessor and not of the lessee, is that frequently goods that may be leased (e.g., refrigerators and other appliances) may become affixed to real estate which the consumer lessee does not own or which is encumbered by the lessee's creditor. In such instances, the lessor's interest will come into conflict with that of the owner or encumbrancer of the real estate. Section 2A-309(5) adds a special rule for a lessor of "readily removable replacements of domestic appliances," subject to a consumer lease, giving the lessor priority over the conflicting interest of the owner or mortgagee of real property, regardless of whether the lessor has perfected its interest by a fixture filing, if the lease contract is enforceable before the goods become fixtures. This rule recognizes the reality that the value to a real estate owner or mortgagee of readily removable domestic appliances is relatively minimal compared to the value of the same goods to the lessor or (because of its impact on its rental obligations) the lessee.

Article 2A has special disclosure provisions for consumer lessees aimed at ensuring that consumers are aware of critical lease terms. For example, where the lessee is a consumer or nonmerchant, a clause in a merchant lessor's form prohibiting nonwritten modification of the form must be separately signed by the lessee. § 2A-208(2). This is a typical disclosure clause aimed at assuring that the lessee knows that oral modifications will not be effective. Another "disclosure" provision requires that any language in a consumer lease which prohibits the transfer of an interest of a party under the lease, or makes such transfer an event of default, must be "specific" and "conspicuous." § 2A-303(7); see Chapter 6.B.4. infra for a discussion of the term "conspicuous." Moreover, a consumer lease cannot be a finance lease unless the lessee either (i) receives an accurate and complete statement summarizing the lessor's rights under the supply contract, (ii) approves the lessor's supply contract as a precondition to the lease's effectiveness, or (iii) receives a copy of the lessor's supply contract before signing the lease. § 2A-103(1)(l)(iii) [§ 2A-103(g)].

Often, there are also special statute-of-frauds provisions for consumer leases. California, Florida, South Dakota, and Utah have amended the Code's statute-of-frauds provision, § 2A-201, to strengthen the writing requirement in consumer leases. In those states, oral nonconsumer leases involving less than $1,000 (as provided in the uniform version) are enforceable; consumer leases must be in writing in every instance. In addition, New York has enacted a new subsection clarifying that the more informal writing requirements of § 2A-201 override the more restrictive provision of its General Obligations Law.

Article 2A also has special rules concerning jurisdiction and venue for consumer leases. The governing law of a consumer lease is limited to the law of the jurisdiction where the "lessee resides at the time the lease agreement becomes enforceable or within 30 days thereafter," or where "the goods are to be used." § 2A-106(1). This protects the lessee from having to deal with the law (and possibly the lawyers) of a distant jurisdiction. For the same reason, the parties to a consumer lease may not choose "a forum which would not otherwise have jurisdiction over the lessee," so that by signing the lease, the consumer lessee does not subject itself to suit in an inconvenient jurisdiction. § 2A-106(2).

Article 2A expands the notion of unconscionability so that consumer lessees have additional remedies in the event of an unconscionable contract or conduct. The court may grant "appropriate relief" if the lease contract (or any clause) has been induced by unconscionable conduct, or if such conduct occurs, in collecting a claim, under a consumer lease. § 2A-108(2). "Appropriate relief" may include the award of attorney's fees to the lessee. Consumers should, however, be alert as courts may also award attorneys' fees to the lessor if the lessee knowingly submits a groundless claim. § 2A-108(4)(b). Indeed, Article 2A goes even farther than Article 2 by excluding the word "commercial" from the statute directing the court to examine, on its own motion or by motion of a party, whether a lease is unconscionable. Compare § 2A-108(3) and § 2-302(2). Furthermore, subsection 2 is not intended to be an exclusive remedy. A wronged lessee could sue under both 2A and another legal theory—such as usury or tortious debt collection. Finally, § 2A-503(3) declares that a limitation of the lessee's consequential damages for injuries resulting from consumer goods is prima facie unconscionable. This provision includes "limitation, alteration, or exclusion of consequential damages." Where the loss is "commercial," however, there is no such presumption of unconscionability even in a consumer lease. §§ 2A-108(3) and 2-302(2).

It should be noted that consumer leases may be subject to other law outside Article 2A and the UCC. In addition to general consumer law, there is the Uniform Consumer Leases Act, the federal Consumer Leasing Act, and Regulation M promulgated by the Federal Reserve Board under the latter statute.

B. Finance Leases

In the classic leasing transaction, the lessor of the goods (e.g., an equipment vendor) is also the supplier of the goods, hence the basic rules of Article 2A place responsibility on the lessor for the quality of the goods. Where a third party supplies the goods, however, and the lessor (who acquires the goods at the request of the lessee solely to lease them to the lessee) only finances the transaction, placing responsibility on the lessor for such basic elements as the quality of the goods is illogical. There are in effect two different transactions: the supply contract between the supplier and the lessor, under which the lessor acquires the goods; and the lease contract between the lessor and the lessee, under which the lessee acquires the use and possession of the goods from the lessor. Article 2A refers to this type of tripartite lease as a "finance lease" and sets forth a different set of rules for such transactions. § 2A-102(1)(l).

Given the unique nature of these tripartite transactions and the special rules which Article 2A applies to such transactions, the definition of a finance lease is crucial. To qualify as a finance lease, a lease must satisfy three requirements. First, the lessor must "not select, manufacture, or supply the goods." § 2A-103(1)(g)(i). Only in such an instance would it be desirable to shield the lessor from any liability for the quality of the goods. Second, the lessor must acquire its rights in the goods "in connection with the lease," § 2A-103(1)(l)(ii). If the lessor already owned the goods or had rights in the goods independent of the lease transaction, the necessary connection between the lease contract and the supply contract (and with the supplier), which supports imposition of warranty liability on the lessor, would be lacking. Moreover, while imposition of liability on the lessor is not justified where it has dealt with the goods solely at the lessee's request, if the lessor has previously owned the goods the reasons for insulating it from warranty liability evaporate.

Last, one of four procedures must have been followed. These procedures are designed to assure that the lessee, who under a finance lease has no rights against its lessor but is relegated to enforcing the supply contract against the supplier in the event of any defect in the goods, is fully informed of the rights existing under the supply agreement. These four mandatory procedures are aimed at ensuring that the lessee knows (i) what promises or warranties exist under the supply agreement; (ii) what disclaimers exist; and (iii) what limitations or modifications of remedies are included. To that end, § 2A-103(1)(g)(iii) provides that, to qualify as a finance lease, one of the following four procedures must have been followed prior to signing the lease agreement:

(i) before or when it signs the lease, the lessee receives a copy of the supply contract, or "an accurate and complete statement" summarizing the rights provided to the lessor under the supply contract, or (if the lease is not a consumer lease) a notice in specified form from the lessor, stating the lessee's rights with respect to the supply contract;

(ii) the lessee's approval of the supply contract is a condition to effectiveness of the lease;

(iii) before signing the lease, the lessee receives an accurate and complete statement designating the promises, warranties, and limitations or modification of remedies, such as the manufacturer of the goods provided to the lessor; or

(iv) before it signs the lease, the lessee, if the lease is not a consumer lease, is informed by the lessor in writing (or in a record) (a) of the identity of the supplier of the goods (unless the lessee has selected the supplier); (b) that Article 2A entitles the lessee to enforce promises and warranties made about the goods to the lessor, and (c) that the lessee may communicate with the lessor's supplier and receive a statement of the promises, warranties, or disclaimers made.

An example of (i) above would occur when the lessee receives a copy of the supply agreement between the lessor and the supplier, or a letter from the supplier or lessor summarizing the lessor's rights in the supply contract, before the lessee signs that lease. In such instances, the lessee is on notice of the rights it has in the supply agreement. An example of (ii) occurs when the lessee enters into the supply contract and then assigns it to the lessor. Since the lessee in fact negotiated and entered into the supply agreement, it is charged with knowledge of the applicable warranty terms. An example of (iii) would be a supplement to the lease, delivered before the lease is signed, describing the supplier's promises, warranties, and limitations under the supply contract. Again, the notice function is served. Option (iv) could be handled by a lease clause containing the necessary information. Once the lessee knows the identity of the supplier, it can obtain for itself any additional information needed on warranties. Because this option places the burden of inquiry on the lessee, it is unavailable in the consumer lease context. Central to all this is that the lessee in a finance lease is entitled to the benefits of, and is entitled to enforce, the supply contract. § 2A-209.

As with consumer leases, there are several special Code provisions that only apply to finance leases. Most importantly, Article 2A recognizes that the supplier, not the lessor, should be responsible for the quality of the goods. Not only does this result in changes to many of the lease warranty provisions and the grant of a right to the lessee to pursue the supplier on warranty theories despite the absence of privity, but it also requires important reconciliation in the area of remedies.

As the intended user of the goods, the finance lessee is the beneficiary of the supply contract and must look to the supplier of the goods, rather than the lessor, for warranties. § 2A-209. Warranties made by third parties (such as the manufacturer) to the supplier also pass to the finance lessee. These provisions exist because the intended user of the goods (the finance lessee) is the one who should benefit by any warranties made. Giving the lessee rights against the supplier, moreover, compensates for restricting the lessee's traditional rights against the lessor.

Article 2A also insulates the finance lessor from liability for breach of some implied warranties. Under Article 2A, the finance lessor is not responsible for any implied warranties of infringement (§ 2A-211), merchantability (§ 2A-212(1)), or fitness (§ 2A-213), although the finance lessor may still make express warranties, such as that of quiet enjoyment. Finance lessors perform merely a credit function, and play no role in selecting, manufacturing, or otherwise supplying the goods; thus there is no overriding policy for imposing on finance lessors liability for the quality of the goods. Instead, it is the finance lessee who selects both the goods and the supplier. Similarly, a finance lessor is not responsible for any implied warranty of fitness for a particular purpose, because the finance lessee only looks to the supplier's expertise in selecting the goods. Indeed, if the finance lessor becomes involved in selection of the goods, the resulting lease will not qualify as a finance lease under § 2A-103(1)(g)(i).

In finance leases, the risk of loss passes automatically to the finance lessee (§ 2A-219(1)), because a mere financing intermediary should not be responsible for insuring or replacing damaged goods. If a nonconforming tender creates a right to reject, the risk of loss stays with the supplier. § 2A-220(1)(a). At no time does the risk of loss fall on the finance lessor. Finance lessees, like all other lessees, can treat the lease as avoided when a partial casualty loss occurs, but consumer lessees under a finance lease are the only people with the option of accepting the goods with a rental allowance. § 2A-221(b). Where a total casualty loss occurs before delivery, however, any kind of finance lease is avoided.

In finance leases that are not consumer leases, the lessee's promises become irrevocable and independent upon the lessee's acceptance of the goods. § 2A-407. Once the lessor has acquired the goods for the lessee under a supply contract with the supplier, it has completely performed its part of the lease agreement and a nonconsumer finance lessee will be held to its payment obligations. The lessee must perform even if the lessor's post-acceptance performance is in breach of the lease agreement (e.g., where the lessor itself or its collateral assignee interferes with the lessee's quiet enjoyment). Even though it is bound to the lease agreement, the commercial finance lessee may pursue its other remedies, including an action for damages against the supplier (for breach of its warranties under the supply agreement) or the lessor (for breach of quiet enjoyment). § 2A-209.

Thus, a finance lessor gets the benefits of a "hell or high water" clause even if no such clause is written in the agreement. Nonetheless, it has become commonplace to insert hell or high water clauses in finance lease agreements because of the possibility that a court will deny that the agreement is a finance lease. Comment (g) to § 2A-103 admonishes that, unless the lessor is confident that a particular transaction will qualify as a finance lease, the lease agreement should include a hell or high water clause and other provisions giving the lessor the benefits created by the special Article 2A provisions for finance leases. For instance, such a hell or high water clause could state that:

Lessor and Lessee agree that this Lease constitutes a net lease and that Lessee's obligations hereunder are absolute and unconditional and that all amounts due hereunder, and all other Lessee obligations shall not be subject to any abatement, reduction, setoff, defense, counterclaim, interruption, deferment, or recoupment for any reason whatsoever, and that such payments, and all other Lessee obligations, shall be and continue to be payable and performed in all events.

Another protection afforded finance lessors is a finance lessee's inability to revoke its acceptance of nonconforming goods that the lessee has accepted with knowledge of the nonconformity.

§ 2A-516(2). To allow revocation would essentially force the goods back to the finance lessor (who has no use for them and no ready means for their disposal) even though the supplier (not the lessor) was the party causing the breach. A finance lessee may revoke acceptance only if the nonconformity substantially impairs the value of the goods to the lessee and if the lessee failed to discover the nonconformity when accepting the goods because the lessee was reasonably induced to accept the goods based upon the finance lessor's assurances. § 2A-517(1). For example, suppose the Boy Scouts of America, New England Chapter, contracts in July to rent 500 winter sleeping bags for the next five years. During negotiations, the lessor assures the lessee that the bags are rated to -50°F. When the bags arrive in August, the lessee reasonably relies on the lessor's assurances and does not inspect the amount or quality of fill in the bags before accepting. In November, during the first overnight camping trip when the bags are used, the Boy Scouts discover the bags are only rated to 25°F. Because of the lessor's assurances that the bags were suitable for cold weather, the Scouts did not discover the nonconformity until months after acceptance. They may then revoke the previously accepted sleeping bags.

Finally, it is worth noting that the Code has no special rules for situations where the finance lessor is an affiliate of the seller of the goods, an issue left to case-by-case resolution.

CHAPTER

4

CREATION

Part 2 of Article 2A addresses such contract formation issues as offer and acceptance (§§ 2A-204, 2A-205, 2A-206), the statute of frauds (§ 2A-201), parol evidence (§ 2A-202), and modification (§ 2A-208). Virtually all of these sections are based on comparable provisions of Article 2, with only minor changes to reflect differences in terminology. Thus, the student or practitioner versed in the law of sales will find these creation rules relatively familiar. The drafting of Article 2A preceded the digital age, so practitioners should be aware that in interpreting the writing and signature requirements of that Article, provisions of state enactments of the Uniform Electronic Transactions Act (UETA) or of the federal Electronic Signatures in Global and National Commerce Act (E-Sign), 15 USC § 7001 *et. seq.*, should be taken into account.

A. Offer and Acceptance

There are few formal requirements for the creation of a lease contract: "a lease contract may be made in any manner sufficient to show agreement." § 2A-204. Thus, a lease contract may arise through the conduct of the parties as well as by their exchange of words. It is not necessary that the moment of its making be determined, and the presence of open or omitted terms is not fatal, as long as the parties intended to make a lease contract and there is a basis for giving a remedy. § 2A-204(3). Contracts may be formed even if humans were not directly involved in the formation of the contract. UETA, which would augment the provisions of Article 2A in those states where it has been exacted, clarifies that a contract may be formed electronically: through individuals exchanging electronic messages, through the interaction of electronic agents, or through the interaction of an electronic agent and an individual. UETA § 14(1). This is true even though no individual is aware of or reviewed the electronic agents' actions or the resulting terms and agreement. UETA § 14(2).

In the case of an individual dealing with an electronic agent, a contract may be formed if the individual takes steps or makes statements that it is free not to take or make, if it has reason to know that the action or statement will indicate acceptance to the other party or cause it to complete the transaction. *Id.* E-Sign would step in in those states that have not enacted the UETA, but the result would be the same: under E-Sign, a contract may be formed by the action of one or more electronic agents so long as the action of any such electronic agent is legally attributable to the person to be bound. E-Sign § 7001(h). Thus, a person who leases an item over the Internet cannot escape liability by claiming that a website lacks the capacity to contract.

If it is necessary to resort to an offer and acceptance analysis, the rules of Article 2A are virtually identical to the more familiar contract formation rules of Article 2. Unless the offeror unambiguously indicates otherwise, an offer may be accepted "in any manner and by any medium reasonable" under the circumstances. § 2A-206(1). If the offeree accepts the offer by beginning performance, however, the offeror must be notified within a reasonable time or it may treat the offer as having lapsed. § 2A-206(2). Although under common law an offer may be withdrawn up to the moment of acceptance, under Article 2A an offeror who is a merchant may make an irrevocable or "firm" offer if the offer is in a signed writing or record which by its terms gives assurances that it will be held open, despite the absence of any consideration. § 2A-205. The offer will be irrevocable for the stated period of time or a reasonable time not to exceed three months. *Id.*

The biggest departure from the contract formation provisions of Article 2 is the omission of the "battle of the forms" provision of § 2-207. When battle of the forms cases arise in the leasing context, i.e., there is an exchange of forms with conflicting terms and the court must determine whether a contract was formed and if so on what terms, courts will undoubtedly be faced with the issue of whether to apply Article 2 by analogy. The "analogy" argument is not necessarily persuasive. The drafters of Article 2A purported to follow the provisions of Article 2, some might say slavishly, unless the sales provisions were deemed too objectionable to be carried over; this may well be the rationale for the omission of § 2-207 in the leasing context and it demonstrates the contradiction inherent in the analogy argument. The "battle of the forms provision" has received extensive criticism over the past fifty years; the failed 2003 amendments extensively revised the provision. The UNIDROIT Convention on the International Sale of Goods and the UNIDROIT Principles of International Commercial Contracts each contain major departures from the "battle of the forms" rules of Article 2. Thus, § 2-207 undoubtedly falls into the category of Article 2 provisions affirmatively rejected in the drafting of Article 2A.

There have been few reported cases relating to lease contract formation. In *Cobra Capital, LLC v. RF Nitro Communications*, 266 F.Supp.2d 432 (M.D.N.C. 2003), a "lease financing proposal" that was "subject to the approval" of one of the purported parties, and that provided for refund of monies paid if either party did "not consummate the transaction," was found not to be a binding contract. In *Fairbrook Leasing, Inc. v. Mesaba Aviation*, 295 F.Supp.2d 1063 (D.Minn.2003), a "term sheet" which failed to provide for all material terms nonetheless was deemed to be a binding contract because it was sufficiently "definite" under Section 2A-204(3) (covering situation where "one or more terms are left open, [but the] lease contract does not fail for indefiniteness").

B. Statute of Frauds

Historically, American law has required a signed writing before certain kinds of contractual undertakings would be enforced. Although this writing requirement, or statute of frauds, has been eliminated in a number of areas, Article 2A continues to impose a writing requirement for all leases. The one exception to the requirement of a signed record (or satisfaction of that requirement in another fashion) is those leases where the total payments to be made under the lease, excluding renewal or purchase option provisions, are less than $1,000. § 2A-201(1)(a).

For a lease not under the threshold amount to be enforceable, the record [or writing] must (i) be signed by the party against whom enforcement is sought (or its agent), (ii) be sufficient to indicate a lease contract was made, (iii) describe the leased goods, and (iv) set out the lease term. § 2A-201(1)(b). Although a record is not insufficient merely because it omits or misstates a term, if the lease term as written is incorrect (e.g., it says ten months instead of twenty months), the lease is not enforceable beyond the term stated in the record. § 2A-201(3). Similarly, if the quantity of the leased goods is misdescribed (one loader instead of two), the lease is unenforceable beyond the quantity stated in the record [or writing]. *Id.*

Article 2A's statute of frauds provision does contain a list of three situations where objective evidence is arguably present that supports the claim of an alleged lease and the statute of frauds record requirement is deemed satisfied. First, if the goods are specially manufactured or obtained for the lessee, and cannot be released or sold in the ordinary course of the buyer's business, then the lease is enforceable if the lessor "has made either a substantial beginning of their manufacture or commitments for their procurement." § 2A-201(4)(a). Second, the lease is enforceable if the person against whom enforcement is sought admits, in "a pleading, testimony or otherwise in court" that it was made, § 2A-201(4)(b), but the lease is not enforceable beyond the quantity admitted. § 2A-201(5)(b); the section is vague as to whether that statement must be under oath. Third, the lease is enforceable, notwithstanding the lack of a record [or writing] stating the quantity of the goods, with respect to those goods already received and accepted by the lessee. § 2A-201(4)(c).

The protection of the last exception is, however, limited, as even though the quantity of goods may not be in a writing, there still must be a lease agreement and the term of the lease must be in writing under the statute of frauds. This is demonstrated by *In re Munroe*, 183 B.R. 667 (Bankr. D.R.I. 1995). There, a bankrupt company had possession of goods but, because a lease contract or sales contract had never been executed, the company was not permitted to assert the existence of an oral lease against the lessor.

The current official text does not address the interrelationship between the statute of frauds in § 2A-201 and the more general statute of frauds provision that exists in all states. The 2003 Amendments added a new provision to the statute of frauds clarifying that if a lease contract is enforceable under § 2A-201, it is not rendered unenforceable under the more general state statute of frauds merely because it is not capable of being performed within one year, but these amendments have been withdrawn. Nonetheless, Connecticut and New York have nonuniform amendments to this section that reach the same result, and there is a good argument that even without such amendments, the specific provisions of § 2A-201 displace the more general provisions of other law.

Because the Article 2A statute of frauds provision parallels that in Article 2, it can be assumed that cases under the comparable provision of Article 2 will be relied upon in interpreting § 2A-201, including those cases dealing with the availability of estoppel as a common law exception to the writing requirement.

C. Electronic Contract Formation

The inability to pass the 2003 Amendments to Article 2A, which contained provisions designed for the modern electronic era, leaves Article 2A subject to UETA if enacted in the forum state or to the federal E-Sign 15 U.S.C. § 7701 *et. seq.* The thrust of UETA and E-Sign are that a record or a signature may not be denied legal effect or enforceability solely because it is in electronic form, nor may a contract be denied legal effect or enforceability solely because an electronic record was used in its formation. UETA § 7; E-Sign § 7001(a). The language "may not be denied legal effect or enforceability solely because" electronic means were used was deliberately chosen because it recognizes that there may be other reasons why the record, signature, or contract will not be enforced. An example might be a contract entered into by reason of duress. This legislation clarifies, however, that Article 2A does not require the use or processing of electronic records or electronic signatures.

A second major issue regarding electronic contracting, § 2A-223, deals with the attribution of electronic records and signatures. An electronic record or electronic signature is attributed to a person (UETA § 9): if it was the act of that person (UETA § 9); if it was an act of that person's electronic agent; or if the person is otherwise legally bound by the act, for example, under the applicable law of agency.

The third major contract formation provision in UETA deals with electronic communication, stating that a contract may be formed by the interaction of electronic agents of the parties, and even if no individual is aware of its receipt. UETA § 14.

CHAPTER

5

INTERPRETATION

Assuming the parties have entered into an enforceable leasing agreement, Article 2A sets forth a framework for interpreting that agreement, including rules on (i) how the various terms of the agreement are to be construed; (ii) the extent to which parol evidence (or evidence outside a written agreement) may be used to supply terms of the agreement; (iii) the implication of a duty of good faith in the interpretation or enforcement of the agreement; (iv) the manner in which the parties may modify terms of the agreement; and (v) when terms of the agreement will not be enforced because they are unconscionable.

A. Rules of Construction

In instances where the parties have expressly agreed upon the terms of their agreement, those terms will control in any dispute between the parties. § 1-303(e)(1) [§ 2A-207(2)]. The Code recognizes, however, that in many instances, even absent express agreement, the terms of the agreement may be found in three additional ways. First, where the agreement calls for repeated performance by either party and the other party acquiesces or fails to object to the manner in which performance is rendered, that course of performance may be used to determine the meaning that the parties give to the terms of the agreement between them. § 1-303(a), (d) [§ 2A-207(1)]. Second, under general Code principles, if the parties have entered into similar transactions prior to the one being considered, their prior conduct in those transactions may demonstrate a course of dealing which again may be used to give content or meaning to the later agreement. § 1-303(b), (d) [§ 1-205]. Third, usage of trade, that is, any practice or method of dealing observed by people in the same place, vocation, or trade, may similarly be used to establish the parties' intentions. § 1-303(c), (d) [§ 1-205(2)-(3)]. This hierarchy (course of performance, course of dealing, and usage of trade) provides a ready solution where a conflict exists between the three and it is impossible to reasonably construe the terms as consistent with one another: course of performance controls course of dealing, and course of dealing controls trade usage. The express terms of the agreement will, however, control all three. § 1-303(e) [§ 2A-207(2)].

B. Parol Evidence

Under the parol evidence rule, terms in a writing which the parties intended as the final expression of those terms are considered established, and cannot be contradicted. § 2A-202. Evidence of supplemental terms may be introduced, unless the court finds that the writing was intended by the parties as the complete and exclusive statement of the terms of their agreement (i.e., a "total integration"). § 2A-202(1)(b). In any event, however, course of dealing and usage of trade may be used to explain or supplement the contract, whether it is partially or completely integrated.

C. Implied Duty of Good Faith

The mandate of the Code is explicit: "[e]very contract or duty within this Act imposes an obligation of good faith in its performance or enforcement." § 1-304 [§ 1-203]. Good faith is a defined term which, under Revised Article 1, means "honesty in fact" and the "observance of reasonable commercial standards of fair dealing in the trade." § 1-201(b)(20); 2A-103(1)(m); under pre-revision Article 1 and the 1990 official text of Article 2A, however, the "fair dealing" standard is limited to merchants. [§ 1-201(19) and § 2A-103(1)(m)]. Contracting parties cannot under any version waive the implied duty of good faith. § 1-302(b) [§ 1-103(3)].

Thus in *Central Funding, Inc. v. CompuServe Interactive Serv., Inc.*, 2003 WL 22177226 (Ohio App. 2003), the court (applying general contract law principles and without citing Article 2A) held that Central Funding, Inc., the lessor of computer equipment, had breached its duty of good faith in its negotiation of a fair market value purchase option of a commercial equipment lease. The lease provided that the lessee would have the option to purchase the equipment at the expiration of the lease term for its fair market value, which was to be mutually determined by lessee and lessor as the price "obtainable in a transaction between an informed and willing user ... and an informed and willing seller." However, Central Funding insisted on using a schedule created at the inception of the lease for use in the event that the lessee wished to purchase the equipment during the initial term of the lease (and thus calculated to allow lessor to recover its equity in the equipment) rather than the price that the equipment would command in the open market. Therefore, the court held that Central Funding had breached its duty of good faith.

D. Modification and Waiver

Article 2A rejects the common law rule that any modification must be supported by consideration to be enforceable. § 2A-208. Moreover, unlike Article 2, there is no "statute of frauds" imposing a writing requirement on certain modifications; according to the drafters, "it is unfair to allow an oral modification to make the entire lease agreement unenforceable," as might be the case if the rentals were increased to over $1,000. § 2A-208, Official

Comment. Nonetheless, the parties themselves may, in a signed lease agreement, exclude any modifications or rescissions except by a signed writing, in essence adopting a "private" statute of frauds. § 2A-208(2). This is consistent with pre-Article 2A law. See *Orix Credit Alliance, Inc. v. Kim*, 909 F. Supp. 216 (S.D.N.Y. 1996) (enforcing a no-oral-modification clause in the lease, even though the lessee claimed to have been orally released from the contract).

Unless both parties are merchants, a no-oral-modification clause contained in a form furnished by a merchant must be "separately signed by the other party." § 2A-208(2). Even where the writing excludes modification except by a signed writing, an attempt at modification may operate as a waiver. § 2A-208(3). That waiver may be retracted by reasonable notification unless the other party has materially changed its position in reliance on the waiver, and enforcement of the strict terms of the agreement would be "unjust." § 2A-208(4). This provision may be of importance to lessors who orally agree to allow the lessee to make payments after the date set in the lease agreement, but then later wish to demand strict compliance with contractual payment dates. *Id.* Such retractions and insistence on strict compliance should be permissible as long as there has been no material change in position by the other party. The lessor may not, however, assert the pre-retraction late payments as contractual breaches.

E. Unconscionability

A key concept, which allows a court to monitor the bargain struck by the parties to determine whether there has been any overreaching resulting in gross unfairness, is the concept of unconscionability found in § 2A-108. The general provision found in § 2A-108(1) is taken almost verbatim from § 2-302, and allows a court to refuse to enforce an unconscionable lease, or any portion thereof, if it "as matter of law finds a lease contract or any clause of a lease contract to have been unconscionable at the time it was made." § 2A-108(1).

For instance, the court in *Advanta Business Services Corp. v. Colon*, 2004 WL 422818 (N.Y. Sup. App. Term. 2004) held that a genuine issue of material fact existed regarding the conscionability of the process of negotiating a finance lease agreement where the lessee was insufficiently proficient in English. Similarly, the court in *Preferred Capital, Inc. v. Warren*, 2003 WL 22515182 (N.Y. Sup. Ct. 2003) found that the defendant-lessee in a finance lease of an ATM machine had sufficiently raised the issues of procedural and substantive unconscionability to defeat plaintiff-finance lessor's motion for summary judgment where the defendant was told by the vendor that she would only be liable for $11 per month, and was not told that if the vendor failed to pay offsets to the finance lessor, the lessee would be liable for the full lease amount. The court found that the defendant's affidavit alleged high-pressure commercial tactics, inequality of bargaining power, deceptive practices, and imbalance in the understanding and acumen of the parties sufficient to raise the issue of procedural unconscionability. The court also found that the inflated price of the ATM lease (total lease payments were $16,000 while retail price of the machine was $4,000) and an unfair termination clause raised the issue of substantive unconscionability. However, the court in *Imaging Financial Services, Inc. v. Graphic Arts Services, Inc.*, 172 F.R.D. 322 (N.D. Ill. 1997), rejected an unconscionability defense based upon an alleged lack of bargaining power in negotiating the terms of a lease. The court, analyzing the lease signed prior to the adoption of Article 2A under New York case law, noted that clauses in commercial contracts are rarely found to be unconscionable. And in *Emlee Equipment Leasing Corp. v. Waterbury Transmission Inc.*, 23 UCC Rep. Serv. 389, 626 A.2d 307 (1993), the court upheld the general validity of finance leases, citing Article 2A and commentary thereon (even though Article 2A had not yet been adopted in the jurisdiction) and rejected an unconscionability challenge to a commercial finance lease even though the lessee was left with no recourse when the equipment malfunctioned, stating that the facts and circumstances did not indicate any inequality of bargaining power or element of unfair surprise.

One major change from the Article 2 approach in the unconscionability provision occurs in the case of consumer leases. Section 2A-108(2) expands the concept of unconscionability in such leases to cover two situations where the lease as written was not unconscionable, but one party acted unconscionably. If the court finds as a matter of law that (i) a lease contract or any clause of a lease contract has been induced by unconscionable conduct, or that (ii) unconscionable conduct has occurred in the collection of a claim arising from a lease contract, the court may grant "appropriate relief." § 2A-108(2). This provision, based on Uniform Consumer Credit Code § 5.108, means that a statement made to induce the consumer to lease the goods, knowing that an integration clause may be invoked later in an attempt to exclude evidence of that statement in a subsequent dispute, may render the lease unconscionable. § 2A-108, Official Comment. Other kinds of unconscionable conduct would include using or threatening to use force or violence in the collection of a claim. *Id.* Thus, § 2A-108(2) provides remedies for such conduct in addition to any remedies otherwise available, e.g., under tort law or debt collection law.

A second major change in the unconscionability provision, again in the case of consumer leases and again based on the Uniform Consumer Credit Code, is the authorization of reasonable attorneys' fees if the court finds unconscionability. In addition, whether or not the lease is a consumer lease, § 2A-108(4)(b) authorizes attorneys' fees against a lessee who brings an unsuccessful unconscionability action that he "knew to be groundless." This award of attorneys' fees does not depend upon the presence of an attorney fee provision in the lease agreement. § 2A-108, Official Comment. Prudent lessees should nonetheless continue to have attorney fee provisions, since they typically cover far more situations than unconscionability claims.

CHAPTER

6

TERMS OF THE LEASE

A. Lessor's Obligations

In general, the lessor's principal obligation under a lease agreement is to provide the goods that have been contracted for. As will be described below, the lessor, as the supplier of the goods, may be held accountable if the goods are subject to claims of another, if the goods are not as described in the lease contract, or if they fail to meet the reasonable expectations of the lessee as set forth in the implied warranty provisions of the Code. There is, however, one important instance where the "general" rules concerning the lessor's obligations do not hold true, and that is in the case of a "finance lessor." A finance lessor, unlike a typical lessor, does not supply the goods, but instead supplies the money with which the goods are acquired. Therefore, as developed more fully above in Chapter 3.B., the finance lessor's obligations are quite different from those described here.

B. Lessor's Warranty Obligations

1. IN GENERAL

When a lessee parts with money for the lease of goods, one of its primary concerns will undoubtedly be that it "gets what it paid for." Initially, the lessee reasonably expects it will acquire the right to use the goods, without interference from others. Additionally, the lessee reasonably expects that the goods will meet any express representations or promises made by the lessor. Or, on another level, the lessee generally expects that, if it leases a car, that the car actually runs. The body of law that protects the lessee's rights to "get what it paid for" is the body of warranty law, and Article 2A sets out the warranties present in lease transactions.

The area of warranties was one of the most litigated areas in leasing prior to the promulgation of Article 2A. In many instances, courts were confronted with arguments that Article 2 on sales should apply since § 2-101 made that article applicable to any "transaction in goods"; other arguments were made that Article 2 should apply by analogy. Article 2A resolves that dispute by adopting warranty provisions (§§ 2A-210 through 2A-216) that parallel the corresponding provisions of Article 2. As noted by the drafters, the "lease of goods is sufficiently similar to the sale of goods to justify this decision." § 2A-101, Official Comment. This is in accord with prior case law where courts overwhelmingly applied the warranty provisions of Article 2 to lease transactions, by outright application of the article (on the theory that leases are transactions in goods) or by analogy. For example, the court in *Walnut Equipment Leasing Co. v. Moreno*, 643 So. 2d 327 (La. Ct. App. 1994), applied the "warranty" and "waiver of warranty" provisions in the Pennsylvania version of UCC Article 2 to leases as well.

One general issue relates to whether a lessee has the right to continue using nonconforming equipment, on the theory that it is mitigating its damages. In *Computer Network, Inc. v. AM General Corp.*, 696 N.W.2d 49 (Mich.Ct.App. 2005), the court ruled that "continued use of goods after revocation is acceptable only in exceptional cases, e.g., where the alternative to continued use was going out of business," *Id.* at 59, or where the lessee ceased using the nonconforming goods as soon as practicable after discovery of the breach of warranty. In that controversy, the lessee failed to utilize an alternative vehicle which was readily available, and continued to use the nonconforming vehicle for the entire lease term during pendency of the litigation. The court found that this use did not constitute valid mitigation of damages.

2. EXPRESS WARRANTIES

Under § 2A-210, which closely follows the express warranty provisions of § 2-312, an express warranty arises whenever the lessor makes any affirmation of fact or promise relating to the goods. § 2A-210(1)(a). Thus, if the lessor states that the machine to be leased will operate at a given speed, an express warranty arises that the machine will indeed operate at that speed. No formal words are necessary to create a warranty, but opinion or commendation alone ("This is a one-of-a-kind offer") does not create an express warranty. § 2A-210(2). Any description of the goods creates an express warranty that the goods conform to that description, so if the lease describes the property as a "1,000 pound crane," delivering a 900-pound crane is a breach of that express warranty. § 2A-210(1)(b).

Last, any sample or model creates an express warranty that the goods will conform to that sample or model. § 2A-210(1)(c). The only requirement in each case is that the affirmation of fact, promise, description, or sample or model "is made part of the basis of the bargain." *Id.* Because liability for express warranties is premised on the grounds that the lessor had made statements during the negotiating process for which the lessor should be held accountable, or has through its words (of description) or action (in using a model or sample) held the goods out to have certain characteristics, there is no exclusion of express warranty liability in the case of finance lessors.

Many leases contain a disclaimer of any warranties, express or implied. To the extent that the same document contains a description or statement of fact about the goods, however, it is doubtful that such a disclaimer will be effective. Furthermore, the court in *Ruzzo v. LaRose Enterprises*, 748 A.2d 261 (R.I. 2000) ruled that in consumer leases disclaimers for personal injuries caused by the use of consumer products were unconscionable and, therefore, unenforceable. Although courts are instructed to interpret express warranties and disclaimers as consistent with each other, "to the extent that the construction is unreasonable," the warranties will control over any disclaimer or limitation. § 2A-214. Presumably, this same approach might result in a finding that express warranties through model or sample are similarly nondisclaimable. Disclaimers of express warranties may nonetheless have a definite function. First, to the extent that there are any prior written or oral express warranties, the presence of the disclaimer may bar proof of these warranties under the parol evidence rule. *Id.* Second, the existence of the disclaimer may be used to demonstrate that the statement made by the lessor never became part of the basis of the bargain, and thus is not an express warranty.

Disclaimers of express warranties are more likely to be upheld in finance lease transactions. In *Siemens Credit Corp. v. Newlands*, 905 F. Supp. 757 (N.D. Cal. 1994), the lessor merely arranged financing of the lessee's equipment acquisition, and the statutory finance lease conspicuously and expressly disclaimed all express and implied warranties with respect to the equipment. The court held that such disclaimers purporting to eliminate breach of express or implied warranties are effective in statutory finance leases, even though the lessor and the equipment manufacturer involved were affiliated companies. *Id.*, at 10-11. Thus, the aggrieved lessee's exclusive recourse was against the vendor under the warranty contained in the supply contract.

More recently, in *Direct Capital Corporation v. New ABI Inc.*, 822 N.Y. Supp. 2d 684 (N.Y. Sup. Ct. 2006), the court held that the lessor's disclaimer of warranties, in small type, was not conspicuous. However, because the lease was an Article 2A finance lease, §§ 2A-212 and 2A-213 expressly excluded the implied warranties of merchantability and fitness for a particular purpose. Consequently, the lessee was compelled to continue making rental payments to the finance lessor, while still permitted to pursue its claims against the equipment vendor.

3. IMPLIED WARRANTIES

a. Warranty against Interference. A lessee who leases property is not concerned that the lessor's title to the property is perfect; instead, its concern is that no one will interfere with its right to possess and use the property during the lease term. Although the implied warranty of quiet possession was abolished with respect to sales in Article 2, Article 2A in § 2A-211(1) reinstates the warranty of quiet possession with respect to leases but renames it a warranty against interference. The Official Comments to the 1990 text noted that "[i]nherent in the nature of the limited interest transferred by the lease—the right to possession and use of the goods—is the need of the lessee for protection greater than that afforded to the buyer." § 2A-211, Official Comment. Thus, there is implied in every lease transaction a warranty by the lessor that no person holds any claim to or interest in the goods, arising from any act or omission of the lessor, which will interfere with the lessee's enjoyment of its leasehold interest. § 2A-211(1). In addition, lessors who are not finance lessors also warrant that no person holds any claim to or interest in the goods, or any such "colorable" claim or interest, not attributable to the lessor's own acts or omissions that will interfere with the lessee's right of quiet enjoyment. § 2A-211(1).

One example of how this warranty may be breached is instructive for lessors. Assume that the lessor leases a piece of equipment to the lessee. Unknown to the lessee, the equipment is subject to a security interest held by a bank. At this stage, there has been no breach of the warranty against interference since perfect title is not warranted. If, however, as the result of the lessor's breach of its agreement with the bank, the bank repossesses the equipment during the lease term, depriving the lessee of the right to possess and use the property, a breach of the warranty against interference has occurred. Thus, the court in *Bancorp Group, Inc. v. Michigan Conference of Teamsters Welfare Fund*, 585 N.W.2d 777 (Mich. Ct. App. 1998), held that a lessor's warranty against interference under § 2A-211(1) was breached when "the city acquired a claim or interest in the goods by virtue of [the lessor's] failure to pay its personal property taxes" and the judgment explicitly gave the city a right to seize the goods.

The implied warranty against interference may be disclaimed, as long as the disclaimer meets the requirements of § 2A-214: the disclaimer must use specific language (presumably referring specifically to the warranty against interference), it must be in a writing, and it must be conspicuous. § 2A-214(4). In this regard it should be noted that the warranty against interference, like the warranty against infringement (discussed below), is not characterized by the Code itself as an "implied warranty"; consequently, "as is" language which, under the Code, "makes it plain that there is no implied warranty," would not be sufficient to disclaim these warranties. § 2A-214. The warranty against interference may be excluded if the circumstances (including course of performance, course of dealing, or usage of trade) give the lessee reason to know that the goods are leased subject to another's claim, § 2A-214(4), or that the lessor purports to transfer only such rights as it or a third party may have. Note that it is not enough that the lessee have reason to know of the existence of another claim; the lessee must have reason to know that the goods are subject to that other claim. *Id.*

b. Warranty against Infringement. A lessor who is a merchant regularly dealing in goods of the kind impliedly warrants that the goods are delivered free of any infringement claims. § 2A-211(2). In a warranty against infringement, a lessor warrants that the lessee's interests will not be marred by any third-party claim of patent or trademark infringement concerning the leased property. This warranty is not made by a finance lessor; the finance lessee, however, who has the benefits of all warranties contained in the supply contract (including, presumably, the warranty against infringement in that contract) may hold the supplier accountable if infringement claims arise. § 2A-209(1). Where, however, the lessee has furnished the specifications for the goods, and compliance with those specifications results in an infringement claim, it is ultimately the lessee, not the lessor, who is liable. § 2A-211(3).

As with the implied warranty against interference, the implied warranty against infringement may be disclaimed, as long as the disclaimer meets the requirements of § 2A-211(4) [§ 2A-214]: the disclaimer must use specific language, it must be in a record [or writing], and it must be conspicuous. § 2A-214(2). Again, an "as is" disclaimer would be insufficient for these purposes. Alternatively, the warranty is excluded by a showing that the lessee had reason to know that the goods were leased subject to that claim. *Id.*

c. Warranty of Merchantability. The implied warranty of merchantability provisions are an attempt to protect the reasonable expectations of the lessee as to what it is leasing, even in the absence of any express statements or promises. That warranty, found in § 2A-212, is taken almost verbatim from the merchantability provisions of Article 2 (§ 2-314). In every lease where the lessor is a merchant with respect to goods of the kind involved in the transaction, there is an implied warranty that the goods, inter alia:

(i) would pass without objection in the trade under the contract description;

(ii) if fungible, are of fair average quality;

(iii) are fit for the ordinary purposes for which goods of that type are used;

(iv) are of even kind, quality, and quantity (within the contract description);

(v) are adequately contained, packaged, and labeled;

(vi) conform to any promises or affirmations made on the container or label. § 2A-212(1)-(2).

Other implied warranties may arise from course of dealing or usage of trade. §§ 2A-212(3), 1-303 [§ 1-205].

The implied warranty of merchantability may be disclaimed, subject to the requirements of § 2A-214. The disclaimer must mention "merchantability," be in a writing, and be conspicuous. The warranty may not be disclaimed orally. § 2A-214(2).

Thus in *Voelker v. Porsche Cars North America, Inc.*, 353 F.3d 516 (7th Cir. 2003), superseding 348 F.3d 639 (7th Cir. 2003), the court found that the lessor was shielded from liability under a theory of implied warranty of merchantability where the consumer automobile lease contained a conspicuous disclaimer of warranties which was in bold type and which specifically mentioned merchantability.

In contrast, a disclaimer (not capitalized or boldface) that was listed among one of many numbered items in a lease was struck down as inconspicuous in *In re Bailey v. Tucker Equipment Sales, Inc.*, 510 S.E.2d 904 (Ga. Ct. App. 1999). Further, the court in *Labella v. Charlie Thomas, Inc.*, 942 S.W.2d 127 (Tex. App. 1997), held that a conspicuous warranty disclaimer specifically mentioning merchantability may nonetheless be unenforceable where the warranty's reference to "purchase" and "sale" rather than "lease" created a factual issue as to whether the lessee had the required notice of the disclaimer.

d. Warranty of Fitness for Purpose. An implied warranty that the goods will be fit for the lessee's particular purpose arises if, at the time the lease is made, two requirements are met: (i) the lessor has reason to know of any particular purpose for which the goods are required; and (ii) the lessor has reason to know that the lessee is relying upon the lessor's skill or judgment to select or furnish suitable goods. § 2A-213. Thus, if a skier with an old pair of ski boots rents the remainder of her skiing equipment from a ski rental establishment that knows the equipment will be used with the skier's own boots, an implied warranty of fitness may arise that the rented skis and bindings are compatible with those boots. *Ghionis v. Deer Valley Resort Co.*, 839 F. Supp. 789, 791,

24 U.C.C. Rep. Serv. 2d (Callaghan) (D. Utah 1993). The status of the lessor as a "merchant lessor" is irrelevant to the creation of this warranty, although a finance lessor is excluded from the coverage of this section. § 2A-213. For instance, in *One Stop Pet, Inc. v. Eastern Business Machines, Inc.*, 40 U.C.C. Rep. Serv.2d 497 (Va. Cir. Ct. 1999), the court held that implied warranties of merchantability and fitness for a particular purpose did not apply to finance leases.

For the fitness warranty to be disclaimed under § 2A-214(2), the disclaimer must be in a writing, and be conspicuous.

4. Exclusion or Modification of Warranties

In attempting to disclaim warranties, lessors are well advised to study the requirements for effective disclaimers set out in § 2A-214. Article 2A sets out the manner in which the various warranties may be disclaimed, and compliance with its requirements will give most lessors a "safe harbor" from warranty claims.

- *Implied warranty of merchantability.* A disclaimer must mention "merchantability," be in writing, and be conspicuous to be enforceable. The warranty may not be disclaimed orally. § 2A-214(2).
- *Implied warranty of fitness for purpose.* The disclaimer must be in a record and be conspicuous. *Id.*
- *Implied warranty against interference or infringement.* The disclaimer must use specific language, be in writing, and be conspicuous. § 2A-214(4).

Under § 2A-214(3), implied warranties (except those against interference or infringement) may be disclaimed by "as is" or similar language that makes it plain that there are no implied warranties. The "as-is" disclaimer must be conspicuous; where it is buried in a larger agreement, or is ambiguous, it will not be enforced. For instance, in *Barcelona Equipment, Inc. v. Target Construction, Inc.*, 2012 WL 5866048 (E.D. La. 2012), the lessor's motion for summary judgment was denied where the "as-is" language was "written in the same font used in the document" and there was no bold face or capital letters as were used in other sections of the lease. The court ruled that any disclaimer of the warranty of merchantability must mention merchantability and be conspicuous.

All disclaimers are subject to attack under general contract doctrines such as unconscionability. Thus, in *Oz General Contracting Co., Inc. v. Timesavers, Inc.*, 2012 WL 4344500 (E.D.N.Y. 2012), the court reviewed a disclaimer under New York law which requires that the contract provision be both procedurally and substantively unconscionable. Lacking any evidence of an "atmosphere of haste and pressure," the court upheld the disclaimer of merchantability and fitness for a particular purpose.

Implied warranties may be excluded by conduct as well as words. § 2A-214(1). If the lessee makes a full examination of the goods (or a sample or model) prior to entering into the lease agreement, there is no implied warranty with respect to defects that such an examination should have revealed. § 2A-214(3)(b). The same result follows if the lessee, although requested, refuses to examine the goods. *Id.* A good example is *Driscoll v. Standard Hardware, Inc.*, 785 N.W.2d 805 (Minn. Ct. App. 2010), where the lessee of a mining drill who had used it for one year before exercising its purchase option brought claims against the manufacturer for fraud and breach of warranty. Normally, if a buyer has had ample opportunity (such as one year of possession and use) to inspect the good before purchase, there is no implied warranty. However, in this case the lessee convincingly argued that the drill contained latent defects which could not be determined by such inspection and use, and hence the court ruled that there was no disclaimer of implied warranty.

In addition, implied warranties of merchantability and fitness may be excluded or modified by course of dealing, course of performance, or usage of trade. § 2A-214(3)(c).

5. Conflict of Warranties

When a number of warranties appear to conflict, a court should first try to construe them as cumulative and consistent with one another. § 2A-215. If that fails, the general rule is that the intent of the parties controls which warranty is dominant. *Id.* There are three simple statutory rules to help ascertain intent:

(i) exact or technical specifications control over models, samples, or general language;

(ii) samples control over general language of description; and

(iii) express warranties control over inconsistent implied warranties (other than the warranty of fitness). *Id.*

C. Lessee's Obligations

1. Statutory Duty to Pay Rent

A lessee "must pay rent for any goods accepted in accordance with the lease contract," with due allowance being given for goods rightfully rejected or not delivered. § 2A-516(1). This duty to pay rent, of course, is one of the essential obligations of the lessee, and Article 2A preserves a lessor's claim for rentals even if the underlying agreement omits this essential term. Note, however, that the existence of a lease agreement must still be proved. Furthermore, in the context of finance leases, the court in *In Re First Interregional Advisors Corp.*, 218 B.R. 722 (Bankr. D.N.J. 1997) stressed that only a lessor and its assigns are entitled to rentals after lessee's acceptance of the goods. Thus, a supplier in a finance lease transaction must look to the lessor and not the lessee for payment for the goods absent express agreement obligating the lessee.

2. "Hell or High Water" Clauses

Often in lease contracts, particularly where the lease is in effect a "finance lease," the lessor includes a "hell or high water" clause obligating the lessee to pay rentals despite any defenses the lessee would otherwise have (such as defects in the goods). Courts have continually had to confront the issue of whether such clauses are enforceable, or whether the lessee retains the ability to raise any claims it may have arising from the lease transaction as a defense in an action for the rent. For example, in *Rhythm & Hues, Inc. v. The Terminal Marketing Co.*, 2004 WL 941908 (S.D.N.Y. 2004), the court denied lessee's motion for summary judgment in a case where the lease contained a hell or high water clause. Lessee claimed that because funds were never advanced nor any equipment ever leased, it had no obligation to make payments under the lease (to the assignee of the lessor). The court held that the lease's unambiguous language creating an unconditional obligation to pay at least created a material issue of fact that prevented a grant of summary judgment in favor of lessee. In *Wells Fargo Bank Minnesota, N.A. v. Nassau Broadcasting Partners LP*, 2003 WL 22339299 (S.D.N.Y. 2003), the court upheld a hell or high water clause in a commercial sale-leaseback and allowed the assignee of the lease to enforce the unconditional obligation to pay even though the lessor had failed to make all funding advances envisioned.

Article 2A specifically provides for the equivalent of a hell or high water clause in instances where there is a nonconsumer finance lease. § 2A-407(1). In such leases, the lessee's promise to pay becomes "irrevocable and independent upon the lessee's acceptance of the goods." Thus, in *Leaf Financial Corp. v. ACS Services, Inc.*, 2010 WL 1740884 (Del. Super. Ct. 2010), the court granted summary judgment in favor of the lessor of a bundled equipment and software system, where the lease expressly stated that it was an Article 2A finance lease and required the lessee to notify the lessor within seven days of installation if it wanted to reject the system. Because the lessee was deemed to have accepted the system and the lease was a finance lease, the lessee's obligations became irrevocable even if the system was defective.

Similarly, in *National City Commercial Capital Co. v. Becker Real Estate Services, Inc.*, 885 N.Y.S.2d 173 (Sup. Ct. 2009), the lessor was granted summary judgment for the accelerated balance due under the lease, plus late charges, where the lease contained a hell or high water clause and the lessee (in its executed delivery and acceptance certificate) had acknowledged that the lease was a finance lease governed by Article 2A. Because the lessee also had made eight rental payments, its allegation of defective equipment and fraud in the inducement were unavailing. In *CN Funding, LLC v. Ensig Group, Ltd.*, 860 N.Y.S.2d 34 (App. Div. 2008), the court was confronted with a lease that did not qualify as a finance lease under section 2A-103(1)(g), although the parties had expressly agreed to treat the contract as such and included a hell and high water clause requiring lessee to pay even if the vendor failed to deliver the goods; the clause was held to be enforceable. *GreatAmerica Leasing Corp. v. Star Photo Lab, Inc.*, 672 N.W.2d 502, 51 U.C.C. Rep. Serv. 2d 1133 (Iowa Ct. App. 2003), in upholding a hell or high water clause in a finance lease despite the lessee's dissatisfaction with the equipment, noted that courts have uniformly upheld the validity of hell or high water clauses.

And in *Jet Acceptance Corp. v. Quest Mexicana, S.A. de C.V.*, 2010 WL 2651641 (N.Y. Sup. 2010), the court granted summary judgment in favor of the lessor under four substantially identical leases which contained a hell or high water clause and cross-default provisions. When the lessee stopped making rental payments under the first lease, claiming that the aircraft was not in "delivery condition," and refused to accept the second and third aircraft when tendered, the court ruled that hell or high water clauses are "respected and enforced" and used the cross-default clause to excuse the lessor from having to deliver the fourth aircraft. These decisions illustrate the importance to the lessor of requiring the lessee to execute and deliver an acceptance certificate, in order to overcome challenges to the hell or high water nature of the lessee's obligations.

However, there are limits to enforceability of hell or high water clauses. The court in *Colonial Pacific Leasing Corp. v. J.W.C.J.R. Corp.*, 977 P.2d. 541, 545 (Utah Ct. App. 1999), interpreted "accepted" to include a "reasonable time to inspect" the goods. Such a "reasonable time" includes an opportunity to put the product to its intended use and "verify its capability to perform as intended" before a hell or high water clause is triggered. Similarly, the court in *Jaz, Inc. v. Foley & First Hawaiian Leasing, Inc.*, 85 P.3d 1099 (Hawaii Intrmed. Ct. App. 2004), ruled that a lessee was not obligated to make all rental payments after signing an acceptance certificate in connection with a hell or high water master lease because the lessee never received the equipment. The court emphasized the need for the lessee to have reasonable time to inspect the equipment before being deemed to have accepted it. In *Information Leasing Corp. v. GCR Investments, Inc.*, 152 Ohio App.3d 260, 787 N.E.2d 652 (Ohio Ct. App. 2003), the court stated that the requirement that the lessee be given a reasonable time to inspect the goods cannot be circumvented.

Another vulnerability may arise if an assignee, seeking to enforce a lease, is found to be complicit in or possessed of knowledge of the lessor's scheme to defraud the lessee. This generally involved a high burden of proof. For instance, in *AT&T Credit Corp. v. Transglobal Telecom Alliance, Inc.*, 966 F.Supp. 299 (D.N.J. 1997), the court upheld the validity of a hell or high water clause in a finance lease contract and rejected the lessee's defense that a "close connection" existed between the lessor and supplier, noting that Article 2A "creates no special rule where the lessor is an affiliate of the supplier." Similarly, in *McNatt v. Colonial Pacific Leasing Corp.*, 472 S.E.2d 435 (Ga. Ct. App. 1996), aff'd in part and rev'd in part, 486 S.E.2d 804 (Ga. 1997), the court rejected a fraud in the inducement defense to a hell or high water obligation in a finance lease made prior to the state's adoption of Article 2A of the UCC, holding that such a defense is only applicable when there exists an agency relationship between the lessors and the alleged perpetrators of the fraud. In a bundled contract involving lease of equipment and provision of maintenance services, the court in *Harte-Hanks Direct Marketing/Baltimore, Inc. v. Varilease Technology Finance Group, Inc.*, 299 F.Supp.2d 505 (D. Md. 2004) permitted the assignee to claim for rentals under a hell or high water clause, where it had not assumed any duty to provide maintenance services under the contract. And the court in *Citicorp Vendor Finance, Inc. v. MedTech Center, Inc.*, 2004 WL 136362 (Cal. App. 2d District 2004), held that there must be a strong showing of false representation before a fraud in the inducement claim can be used to void a hell or high water clause.

Furthermore, the court in *First Bank National Ass'n v. Scripps Howard, Inc.*, 1995 WL 548845 (S.D.N.Y. 1995), held that a hell or high water clause of a lease assigned by the lessor to First Bank applied to a forty-eight-month lease despite the existence of a separate agreement between the lessor and lessee entered into concurrently that allowed the lessee to terminate the lease after thirty-six months. Because First Bank as assignee was unaware at the time of assignment of any different terms in the thirty-six-month lease, the court upheld the hell or high water clause of the lease and barred any action against the assignee arising from the thirty-six-month lease or the separate termination agreement.

If there is an effective hell or high water clause (or there is a finance lease), but defects in the leased equipment surface during the lease term, the lessee will still be obligated to pay its rental payments to the lessor, despite the defense of defective goods. The lessee's recourse is limited to potential claims against the supplier.

In consumer lease cases, or ones involving nonfinance leases, Article 2A is silent on whether the lessee's promise to pay may nonetheless be made irrevocable by the lease contract itself, and such matters will continue to be decided on the facts of each case. § 2A-407, Official Comment 6. But there now exists a long line of decisions which have validated contractual hell or high water clauses, at least in the nonconsumer context. For instance, in *C & J Vantage Leasing Co. v. Wolfe*, 795 N.W.2d 65 (Iowa 2011), the court ruled that the parties to a nontrue lease (which contained a $1 purchase option) could agree to a contractual hell or high water clause and that such provisions should be granted full effect. Nevertheless, the court observed that such a clause would not bar lessee claims and defenses that relate, for instance, to fraud in the inducement, mutual mistake, and unconscionability. Similarly, in *Colorado Interstate Corp. v. CIT Group/Equipment Finance, Inc.*, 993 F.2d 743 (10th Cir. 1993), the Tenth Circuit affirmed the validity of a traditional hell or high water clause in a nonfinance lease despite a breach of the lessee's quiet enjoyment. The court also rejected the lessee's argument that the merchant/nonmerchant distinction is relevant in nonfinance leases for determining the enforceability of such clauses.

However, in *Mercedes-Benz Credit Corp. v. Lotito*, 703 A.2d 288 (N.J. Super. Ct. 1997), a New Jersey appellate court upheld a breach of warranty defense in a consumer lease that contained a disclaimer of all warranties and a hell or high water clause. In an attempt to protect consumers from an "inequality in bargaining power" and the "pressures attendant to an adhesion contract," the court ruled that because of a "sufficiently close relationship between the seller, the manufacturer, and the lessor," a breach of warranty defense against the lessor could not be disclaimed by contract. In that case, the leasing company was closely affiliated with the manufacturer, the distributor, and the vehicle dealer. It created the lease form, authorized personnel at the dealerships to execute the leases "essentially on its behalf," and had "extensive" knowledge of "the terms of the underlying sale agreement."

3. OBLIGATION TO RETURN

As noted earlier, the distinguishing characteristic of a true lease is the right of the lessor to a residual interest in the goods. Upon the expiration of the lease, the lessor has the right to possess and control the goods; if such a right is absent, the lease is not a "true lease." Surprisingly, despite the importance of the lessor's right to the goods upon expiration of the lease, Article 2A itself does not impose any obligation on the lessee to return the goods when the lease is over. A moment's reflection, however, clears up this apparent inconsistency. The lessor's rights and interest in the goods do not depend upon the lease agreement for their existence; all the lease does is grant the lessee a temporal right in the goods. Nonetheless, most leases themselves spell out the return obligation, and that obligation is inherent throughout the provisions of Article 2A.

D. Risk of Loss

In the event of loss or destruction of the goods, the general rule is that the risk of loss is on the lessor, assuming, of course that the loss was not caused by any wrongful act of the lessee. § 2A-219. Although this may seem surprising, since the lessee is in possession of the goods and better able to guard against their loss, the comments explain that this "reflect[s] current practice in lease transactions." § 2A-219, Official Comment.

There are two situations in which the general rule does not apply: (i) where the parties have agreed otherwise, as is often the case in longer-term, commercial leases; and (ii) in the case of a finance lease, where the risk of loss automatically passes to the lessee. § 2A-219. Where the risk of loss is to pass to the lessee, Article 2A sets out specific rules for when that risk of loss passes. § 2A-219(2). Furthermore, default by the lessor may change the allocation of the risk of loss under § 2A-220.

The risk of loss is distinguishable from a determination of who has an insurable interest in the goods. In most circumstances, both parties have such an interest. The lessee obtains an insurable interest upon identification of existing goods to the lease contract, allowing it to protect its leasehold interest. §§ 2A-218(1), 2A-217. The lessor, because of its reversionary interest in the goods, retains an insurable interest in the goods until an option to buy has been exercised by the lessee, thereby destroying that reversionary interest. § 2A-218(3).

Recognizing that both parties (lessor and lessee) have an insurable interest merely reflects the reality that loss or destruction of the goods harms both the lessee (who has bargained for their use and possession for the lease term) and its leasehold interest as well as the lessor (who anticipated reacquiring the goods at the end of the lease) and its residual interest.

CHAPTER
7

PERFORMANCE

Part 4 of Article 2A covers issues arising from nonperformance (actual or anticipated) of the lease contract that falls short of a default under Part 5. Much of Part 5 draws not only from similar provisions of Article 2, but also from analogous sections of the federal Bankruptcy Code.

A. Adequate Assurance; Repudiation

Many leases, especially to consumers, are for short terms: a weekend, a week, or a month. There is little that can occur (or of which the lessor will be aware) prior to the expiration date to justify the lessor's repudiating the contract. Yet, during the term of a lease contract for several months or longer, either party may become aware of events that produce concern whether the other party will be able to perform its obligations under the lease. For instance, the lessor may be named a defendant in a large patent infringement lawsuit which, if adversely determined, may undermine the lessee's rights to use the goods, or the lessee may have suffered materially adverse financial results that may adversely affect its ability to pay future rent installments. Prior to the adoption of Article 2A, most leases did not contain the kind of "insecurity" clause common in many loan agreements allowing a lender to declare a default when it deemed itself "insecure"; a party who suspended its future performance risked triggering a default under the lease and incurring damages payable to the other party.

Under § 2A-401, if either party to a lease contract has reasonable grounds for insecurity with respect to the performance of the other party, the insecure party may make a written demand for adequate assurance of due performance. § 2A-401(2). Until the insecure party receives such assurance, it may suspend any performance for which payment has not previously been received, provided that such suspension is commercially reasonable in the circumstances. *Id.* If adequate assurance of performance is not provided within a reasonable time (not to exceed thirty days) after receipt of the demand, such failure results in a repudiation of the lease contract. § 2A-401(3).

Because "adequate assurance" and "commercially reasonable" are not defined in Article 2A, the attorney wishing to utilize these concepts should consider addressing in the lease what situations concern the client and what remedies would be appropriate. For example, the lease may provide that an insecure lessee is given adequate assurance concerning the lessor's solvency when the lessor warrants that no involuntary petitions in bankruptcy have been filed against it. In many instances, attorneys for both lessor and lessee may wish to disclaim any suspension rights not expressly stated in the contract, making it clear that one party, the lessee for example, may not suspend its own performance except in certain agreed upon situations. This would be particularly advisable where the parties intend the arrangement to be a "net" lease. In net leases, the lessee assumes all obligations of maintenance, insurance, and casualty to the goods. Under those circumstances, there is little for the lessor to perform after the leased goods have been delivered, and lessee suspension of performance or cancellation of the contract would be inconsistent with the general understanding of a net lease. Moreover, it should never be "commercially reasonable" to suspend performance under either a common law "hell or high water" lease or a statutory finance lease that is not a consumer lease. In a finance lease, the lessee's promises become irrevocable and independent upon acceptance of the goods. See § 2A-407 (stipulating that the obligations of the lessee are unconditional, and discussed in Chapter 3.B).

Repudiation occurs when (i) an insecure party does not receive adequate assurance of due performance within a reasonable time after demand for such assurance is received, § 2A-401(3), or (ii) one party to a contract indicates through its statements or conduct that it will not perform all or some material part of its remaining obligations under the contract, and the loss of such performance substantially impairs the value of the lease contract to the non-repudiating party. § 2A-402(1). After any such repudiation, the aggrieved party has the following options under § 2A-401:

(i) for a commercially reasonable time, await retraction of the repudiation and assumption of performance by the repudiating party;

(ii) make demand for and await assurance of adequate performance; or

(iii) resort to any right or remedy for default available under the lease contract or Article 2A, in addition to suspending its performance under the lease contract.

The offending party may retract its repudiation up until the point where the aggrieved party has canceled the lease contract, or materially changed its position in reliance on the repudiation, or otherwise indicated that it considers the repudiation final. § 2A-403.

In the context of the typical net commercial lease, or a statutory finance lease, once the goods have been accepted by the lessee, the lessee incurs an irrevocable obligation to pay rent. § 2A-407. Repudiation should similarly not be available in such a situation, and the lease agreement should so stipulate. Where the lessee's "quiet enjoyment" of vital equipment is essential to the bargain, counsel should draft explicit clauses detailing what constitutes breach of such right and its remedies.

For example, a lessee concerned about its quiet enjoyment of the goods might insert the following clause:

> Lessee acknowledges and understands that the terms and conditions of this Lease have been fixed by Lessor in anticipation of its ability to sell and assign its interest in, or grant a security interest under, this Lease and the Equipment to an assignee (the "Assignee"). In the event of any such assignment, however, Lessor shall, so long as Lessee shall not be in default under this Lease and Assignee shall continue to receive all Rent payable under this Lease, require any such Assignee to agree that it will take no action which might result in a disturbance of Lessee's quiet and peaceful possession of the Equipment or Lessee's unrestricted use thereof for its intended purpose. In the event Lessee's quiet and peaceful possession and unrestricted use of the Equipment is disturbed by such Assignee, the Lessee shall continue to pay all Rent and perform all of its obligations under this Lease, and the Lessor shall forthwith provide Lessee with substantially similar Equipment, to Lessee's satisfaction, at absolutely no cost or expense to Lessee (the parties agree that time shall be of the essence for purposes of the foregoing). The Lessor shall also pay, reimburse, indemnify, and hold harmless Lessee for any and all Rent payments and any and all other costs, expenses, losses, or damages whatsoever suffered by Lessee during that period of time commencing upon disturbance of Lessee's quiet and peaceful

possession and unrestricted use of the Equipment and ending at such time as such disturbance has fully and completely ended or at such time as Lessor provides Lessee with replacement Equipment, as set forth above, and such Equipment is installed and fully operational, to Lessee's satisfaction, whichever is earlier.

B. Substitute and Excused Performance

Notwithstanding its provisions for insecurity and repudiation, Article 2A recognizes that strict compliance with the terms of a lease contract is not always possible. In the event of a change in circumstances, Article 2A gives the parties two alternatives: continue the contract using substitute performance or excuse the nondefaulting party from its contractual obligations.

1. SUBSTITUTE PERFORMANCE

Under § 2A-404, if the agreed location, means, or manner of delivery of the goods fail without fault on the part of the lessor, lessee, or supplier, and if a commercially reasonable substitute means of delivery is available, then the substitute delivery method must be tendered and accepted. If because of domestic or foreign governmental regulation the agreed means or manner of payment by the lessee fail, the lessor can stop delivery until the lessee provides a substitute means or manner of payment that is substantially equivalent. § 2A-404(2)(a). Alternatively, if delivery has already occurred, payment by the means or manner provided by such government regulation discharges the lessee's payment obligation unless the regulation is discriminatory, oppressive, or predatory. § 2A-404(2)(b). This section obviously was written to address unforeseen circumstances not covered in the lease. Nonetheless, the possibility that the lessee might have to accept substitute delivery, or that the lessor might have to accept substitute payment called for by a government regulation, suggests that counsel should anticipate such instances, draft around them—and then disclaim any § 2A-404 remedies.

2. Excused Performance

Excuse of the lessee from its contractual obligations is a more serious matter and is permitted only in certain limited instances involving a lessor's or supplier's inability to produce or deliver the goods. Section 2A-405 cautions that mere delay in performance or nonperformance by a supplier or lessor will not constitute a breach of the lease contract (giving rise to remedies for default) if the agreed performance has been made impracticable by either (i) the occurrence of an event whose absence was a basic assumption of the contract, or (ii) compliance in good faith with any applicable governmental regulation or order. § 2A-405(a).

If the lessor's or supplier's capacity to perform is only partially affected, however, then the lessor or supplier is required to allocate delivery of its goods among all customers in a fair and reasonable manner. § 2A-405(b). In addition, the lessor must notify the lessee (and the supplier under a finance lease must notify the lessor and lessee) once it has knowledge of a delay or nonperformance or the need for allocation. § 2A-405(c). In finance leases, however, the duty to notify rests with the supplier rather than the lessor. In such instances of partial nonperformance, in addition to the above notice and allocation requirements, § 2A-406 further permits the lessee, with respect to the affected goods, to terminate the lease contract or, except in the case of a finance lease that is not a consumer lease, to modify the lease contract by accepting any available goods in substitution and making "appropriate adjustments" to future rent payments. If the lessee fails to make such a modification within thirty days of receipt of notice from the lessor, then the lease contract terminates with respect to the affected goods.

The interrelationship between the excuse provisions of § 2A-405 and the remedial provisions of § 2A-406 is interesting. Assume, for example, that a contingency that was reasonably unforeseen by the parties occurs, such as when a terrorist bomb destroys a large quantity of the lessor's inventory, including a portion of the leased goods. The lessee in such a case may terminate the lease contract under § 2A-406, but the lessee would not be able to sue the lessor for the delay in delivery or the nondelivery because § 2A-405 excuses the lessor's performance. Similarly, a lease for the use of motorboat engines would be subject to § 2A-406 relief if the state legislature subsequently passed a law banning the sale or use of a particular kind of engine, and in that case the lessee could terminate a lease of that kind of motorboat engine. Elemental fairness in these situations dictates that the lease not continue as originally intended.

The termination or rental adjustment remedies are, however, serious and parties may have to choose which remedy to pursue. Neither party may wish the lease to terminate automatically, and a lessor may not want to continue the contract at a modified rent, especially if the lease is a hell or high water lease where the lessor has bargained for an absolute lessee obligation to pay a fixed amount. It is preferable for counsel to anticipate what contingencies might really occur, and then draft more specific remedy provisions addressing those contingencies. To avoid unpleasant surprises, the lease should then disclaim any other remedies under Article 2A involving substitute or excused performance.

CHAPTER

8

DEFAULT

A. General Default Rules

1. UNIQUE CHARACTERISTICS OF LEASES

Leases can be viewed as hybrid transactions, bearing characteristics of both sales and secured transactions. The lease is similar
to the sale in that the lessor/vendor has an interest in goods that
passes under the agreement to the vendee. In the event of default
by the vendor during a sales transaction, the vendee wants to
obtain either the goods themselves or the value of the goods. If
the vendee defaults, the vendor wants the value of what was due
under the agreement. The lease is unlike a sale, however, in that
all of the lessor's interest in the goods does not pass to the lessee;
the critical element of a lease is that the lessor retains its residual
interest in the goods (*cf.* § 2A-103(1)(q)), which both needs to be
protected and must be taken into account in the determination of
damages.

In a like manner, a lease also resembles a secured transaction:
the lessee, like the debtor, is in possession and use of goods that,

upon default, the lessor wants back. Unlike a secured transaction, however, the lessor's residual interest in the goods continues even if there is no default; the lessor has the expectation that upon completion of the lease term, it will have the right to possess the goods. Additionally, if there is a default, the lessor—in addition to claiming damages for rent due and unpaid future rent—is reclaiming goods that belong to it, whereas the secured party is foreclosing on its debtor's ownership interest in the goods in order to dispose of the goods and recover unpaid principal and interest on its loan.

Because a lease is a hybrid transaction, the default provisions of Article 2A are in part drawn from the remedies provisions of Article 2, and in part drawn from Article 9 on Secured Transactions. Those remedies may be divided into three categories: the right to cancel the lease agreement; rights regarding the goods themselves; and the right to damages.

2. REMEDIES PROVIDED IN THE LEASE AGREEMENT

At the outset, whether there has been a breach by a lessee or lessor, the general notion of freedom of contract governs, and the parties are free to choose to define what constitutes default, as well as what remedies govern in the event of default. § 2A-501(1), (2). As always, however, there are restrictions on this freedom, such as the prohibition against disclaimers of the obligations of good faith, reasonableness, diligence, and care. § 1-302(b) [§ 1201(3)]. Moreover, a court may refuse to enforce a remedies provision that it finds unconscionable. § 2A-503(2). The Code is explicit that the goal of any remedies provision is to compensate the injured party, not to penalize the breaching party. § 1-305 [§ 1-206]. Thus, the court in *AT&T Capital Leasing Services, Inc. v. Brasch*, 912 F.Supp. 395 (N.D. Ill. 1996) ruled that late charges in an equipment lease were an unenforceable penalty under Illinois law. Rather, AT&T was entitled to interest from the date of each breach at the rate of 12 percent per annum (using the substantive law of Massachusetts in a diversity of citizenship case).

A lease agreement may provide for remedies different from those provided in Article 2A, and the remedies so provided supplement those in the statute, unless the lease remedies are made exclusive. § 2A-501(2). The classic contractual remedy provision in the event of defective goods is a "repair or replacement" provision. Moreover, the agreement may provide that these contractual remedies are the only remedies available, in which case resort to the remedies of Article 2A is barred unless the exclusive remedy fails of its essential purpose. § 2A-503(2). Thus, in the case where repair is the sole and exclusive contractual remedy, but the defect in the goods causes such damage to them that repair is impossible, it can be argued that the repair remedy has "fail[ed] of its essential purpose" and the other remedial provisions of Article 2A are therefore available. *Id.*

The parties may include a provision in their lease agreement setting out the amount of damages to be awarded in the event of default by either party. § 2A-504(1). Given the difficulty of proving damages in many leasing transactions, and the corresponding prevalence of such liquidated damages provisions in lease agreements, the test for determining the validity of such clauses is more flexible than its Article 2 counterpart; liquidated damages provisions may contain either an amount or a formula, but that amount or formula must be reasonable in light of the probable harm that was anticipated at the time the contract was made. *Id.* It is not necessary to show that actual damages would have been difficult to prove, or that the liquidated damages are reasonable compared to the actual harm that resulted, as long as the amount or formula chosen was reasonable at the time of contracting. The Official Comments to § 2A-504 specifically recognize that loss of tax benefits, attorneys' fees, and costs are important factors to be taken into consideration in assessing liquidated damages provisions. § 2A-504.

Thus, *in PacifiCorp Capital, Inc. v. Tano, Inc.*, 877 F.Supp. 180, 184 (S.D.N.Y. 1995), the court upheld a liquidated damages clause that provided for liquidated damages equal to unpaid rent to the date of declaration of default, plus the stipulated loss value of the equipment. That formula "was not 'grossly disproportionate' to the parties' reasonable estimation of the probable loss that would result from a default." Furthermore, the formula does not have to measure damages precisely, so long as it is reasonable. For instance, in *Wiskup v. Liberty Buick Co., Inc.*, 953 F.Supp. 958 (N.D. Ill. 1997), the court upheld the use of the Rule of 78s in computing rebates to the consumer under a liquidated damages clause in a consumer automobile lease even though this method is less favorable to the consumer than the more technically precise actuarial method.

In contrast, in *In re Montgomery Ward Holding Corp.*, 326 F.3d 383 (3rd Cir. 2003), the court held a liquidated damages clause unenforceable where stipulated casualty values included an amount allowing the lessor to realize a profit on the transaction in addition to the present value of the unpaid rent and the present value of the residual value of the equipment. The court emphasized that "no true liquidated damages provision can put the lessor in a position legally superior to the one that it would have occupied had the lease been fully performed," and found that in allowing for a measure of profit in addition to the monthly rental payments, the casualty value stipulated as damages was in fact a penalty clause. *Id.* In *E Plus Group, Inc. v. Panoramic Communications LLC*, 2003 WL 1572000 (S.D.N.Y. 2003), the court emphasized that a liquidated damages clause should not place a lessor in a better position than it would have been in had the lessee fully performed the contract. Thus, a liquidated damages clause may be unreasonable because its formula includes casualty values for the leased equipment which are set substantially above fair market value and because the formula fails to credit the lessee for the amount received by lessor on the sale or re-lease of the goods.

Other courts have similarly been skeptical of liquidated damages clauses that do not give the lessee credit for the lessor's realized resale or re-lease proceeds. In *Carter v. Tokai Financial Services, Inc.*, 500 S.E.2d 638 (Ga. Ct. App. 1998), the court rejected a liquidated damages provision because it allowed for the leased equipment to be repossessed and sold "without any duty to account...for any proceeds with respect to the sale." The court held that such a formula was an unreasonable pre-estimate of probable loss. In *Information Leasing Corp. v. Chambers*, 152 Ohio App.3d 715, 789 N.E.2d 1155 (Ohio Ct. App. 2003), the court refused to enforce an acceleration clause in a finance lease where the damages provision contained no obligation to mitigate damages. Although both Ohio common law and UCC Article 2A imposed a duty on the lessor to mitigate damages upon lessee's breach, here the lessor failed to repossess the equipment and made no effort to sell or re-lease the goods, despite a request by the lessee. Thus the court treated the lessor as having retained the goods, and awarded damages of past due rent plus the present value of future rent due under the lease minus the market value of the equipment. Likewise, in *Preferred Capital, Inc. v. Warren*, 2003 WL 22515182 (N.Y.Supp. 2003), in a case involving a finance lease, the court found that the lessor's failure to accept the return of goods upon lessee's default in payment (and presumably lessor's failure to attempt to sell or re-lease) was a failure to mitigate damages precluding a motion for summary judgment.

Article 2A's recognition that a liquidated damages clause may include a formula rather than simply an amount is an acknowledgement that many leasing agreements choose the formula route. One common liquidated damages formula requires a calculation of (i) past due rentals, plus (ii) the present value of future rentals, plus (iii) the present value of the lessor's residual interest, allowing the lessor to recover the sum of those amounts minus the net proceeds from the lessor's disposition of the goods. A second formula allows the lessor to recover past due rentals, accelerated future rentals, plus the value of the residual interest, but gives a credit to the lessee based on a periodic depreciation of the value of the goods.

Thus, in *Torres v. Banc One Leasing Corp.*, 226 F.Supp.2d 1345 (N.D.Ga. 2002), aff'd, 348 F.3d 972 (11th Cir. 2003), the court upheld the formula for the "early termination charge" in a class action involving consumer automobile leases which consisted of the sum of all current or past due payments at the time of termination of the lease, the sum of the remaining monthly payments on the lease, and the residual value of the vehicle minus unearned rent charges (as opposed to depreciation) included in the remaining monthly payments calculated according to the actuarial method; the formula amount was further reduced by the realized value of the vehicle. Similarly, in *Sun v. Mercedes Benz Credit Corp.*, 254 Ga. App. 463, 562 S.E.2d 714 (Ga. Ct. App. 2002), the court specifically recognized the enforceability of liquidated damages provisions based on a formula in a consumer automobile lease. The court upheld the portion of the formula awarding all past due and to-become-due rent payments, but not that portion giving the lessor one additional month's rent. In the court's view, this extra month's rent would have given the lessor a windfall.

The court in *Winthrop Resources Corp. v. Eaton Hydraulics, Inc.*, 361 F.3d 465 (8th Cir. 2004) upheld a liquidated damages clause based upon predetermined casualty values if such values are reasonable forecasts of the expected damages. However, in applying New York law, the court in *In re Trans World Airlines, Inc.*, 145 F.3d 124 (3rd Cir. 1998), found a provision of a liquidated damages clause that partially used a stipulated termination value to determine damages to be a penalty or forfeiture and, despite being freely negotiated, unenforceable. The clause made lessee liable for the difference between a stipulated termination value and either the fair market rental value or fair market sale value in addition to lessee's liability for unpaid monthly rentals.

More recently, *GATX Corp. v. Appalachian Fuels, LLC*, 2011 WL 2260695 (E.D. Ky. 2011), awarded the lessor damages equal to the stipulated loss value, together with past due rents and related late charges. Rejecting the contention that the stipulated loss value constituted a penalty, the court observed that such a formula, entered into at the outset of the contract, was designed to compensate the lessor for decline in value of the equipment. The court correctly deducted the actual sale proceeds of the equipment from the damages it awarded.

In addition to actual damages, consequential damages may be liquidated, altered, or excluded in the lease agreement. § 2A-503(3). Such clauses are subject to the test of unconscionability. While such clauses are prima facie unconscionable when personal injury results from consumer goods, there is no such presumption if the loss is commercial. *Id.*

3. CUMULATIVE REMEDIES

The remedies set forth in the lease agreement are in addition to those provided in Article 2A, unless the contractual remedies are specifically made exclusive. § 2A-501(2). Moreover, all the parties' rights and remedies on default, as set forth in the agreement and in Article 2A, are cumulative unless the lease agreement states otherwise. § 2A-501(4). Thus, in *IOS Capital, Inc. v. Jacobi*, 105 S.W.3d 909 (Mo. Ct. App. 2003), the court held that the lessor of office equipment had the right to both repossess the equipment and demand payment of future rental payments in accordance with the acceleration clause of the lease agreement despite the fact that the lessee informed the lessor of the lessee's inability to pay and requested that the equipment be picked up. The court held that because the lessor already had the right to repossess the equipment upon lessee's default under the lease, the lessor's repossession of the equipment did not constitute acceptance of the lessee's offer to cancel the lease and return the equipment, and hence the lessor was entitled to the remaining lease payments under the acceleration clause. Nonetheless, the remedies at law and by contract are subject to the overriding policy that remedies are intended to put the aggrieved party in as good a position as it would have been in had the contract been performed; accumulation of remedies is not available if the injured party will be overcompensated as a result of the accumulation. § 1-305 [§ 1-106].

Courts also have rejected any view that the lessor can enjoy unfettered remedies against a lessee which is in default. For instance, in *Pantoja-Cahue v. Ford Motor Credit Co.*, 872 N.E.2d 1039 (Ill. App. Ct. 2007), the court ruled that the lessor's breaking into a locked garage, in order to repossess the leased vehicle, could be a breach of the peace, entitling the lessee to money damages.

4. NOTICE OF DEFAULT

As a general rule, neither the lessor nor the lessee is entitled to notice of default or enforcement from the other party. § 2A-502. There are certain important exceptions, however. First, the lease agreement itself may require that the nondefaulting party give notice. *Id.* Second, under the Code, if the lessee rejects goods, it must give the lessor notice of the particular defect giving rise to rejection (i) if the lessor had a right to cure and could have cured the defect; or (ii) between merchants, if the lessor makes a written request for a full and final statement in a record of all defects upon which the lessee intends to rely. § 2A-514(1)(a), (b). Failure of the lessee to give that notice will bar the lessee from relying on those defects to justify rejection or establish default. § 2A-514(1). Third, if the lessee has accepted the goods, it must notify the lessor of any defect within a reasonable time after it discovers or should have discovered it; failure to give such notice will bar the lessee from any remedy otherwise arising from such circumstances. § 2A-516(3)(a). Fourth, except in the case of a consumer lease, if the lessee receives notice of litigation for infringement, it must again give notice to the lessor of the action, thereby allowing the lessor to tender a defense, or it will be barred from any remedy otherwise arising from such circumstances. § 2A-516(3)(b). What is interesting is that all of the statutory requirements of notice only apply to notice by the lessee to the lessor. The lessor, on the other hand, is not required to give notice to the lessee of default or enforcement unless the agreement provides to the contrary. § 2A-502.

5. STATUTE OF LIMITATIONS

Article 2A sets forth a four-year statute of limitations for all actions under a lease contract, including breach of warranty or indemnity. § 2A-506(1). The parties may by agreement reduce that period to not less than one year, unless the lease is a consumer lease. *Id.* The cause of action accrues when the act or omission on which the action is based "is or should have been discovered by the aggrieved party." § 2A-506(2).

In *Cadlerock Joint Venture, L.P. v. Remillard*, 67 U.C.C. Rep. Serv. 2d (West) 1043 (N.Y. App. Div. 2008), the court upheld New York's four-year statute of limitations under § 2A-506(1) and rejected the lessor's contention that it was entitled to pursue the lessee guarantor by virtue of the lease provision waiving "any and all rights and remedies conferred" by Article 2A. The decision correctly viewed such waiver, increasingly common in commercial lease transactions, as encompassing substantive provisions (both within and outside Part 5) and not procedural rights (such as the statute of limitations). The court in *ESP Financial Services, LLP v. Vielot*, 794 N.Y.Supp.2d 337 (N.Y. App. Div. 2005), previously had reached the same result, concluding that a statute of limitations was not a right or a remedy awarded by Article 2A.

B. Lessee's Statutory Rights

1. Lessor Defaults

Whether the lessor is in default is determined by (i) the terms of the lease agreement and (ii) Article 2A. § 2A-501(1). Many lease agreements will contain clauses defining what constitutes default by either side. In addition, there are certain events which, under Article 2A, constitute default by the lessor even if not so provided by the agreement: (i) the failure of the lessor to deliver goods in conformity with the lease agreement; (ii) repudiation by the lessor; and (iii) breach of express or implied warranties by the lessor. § 2A-508(1), (4). In the event of default by the lessor, the lessee may proceed to exercise its remedies under the agreement and under Article 2A; there is no requirement that the lessee give notice before resorting to its remedies, unless a notice provision is contained in the lease agreement. § 2A-502.

2. LESSEE REMEDIES

a. In General. An index to the lessee's remedies upon the lessor's default is contained in § 2A-508. They include (i) remedies as to the goods themselves, including the right to reject them, revoke acceptance, or compel specific performance; (ii) rights to recover damages, including the right to recover prepaid rentals; and (iii) rights to cancel the lease contract.

b. Remedies as to the Goods—Forcing the Lessor to Take Back Nonconforming Goods. Where the lessor makes a nonconforming tender of delivery, the lessee is given the right to reject the goods (if it has not yet taken the delivery), or, if it has already accepted the goods, it may opt to revoke its acceptance of the goods. § 2A-509(1). The right to reject arises whenever there is a nonconforming tender, regardless of how minor that nonconformity is. Despite the superficially unequivocal nature of the right to reject, the lessor is given the right to cure a nonconforming tender or delivery under certain circumstances. § 2A-513(1)-(2). For instance, the lessor or supplier can seasonably notify the lessee of its intention to cure and then deliver conforming goods before the original deadline for delivery passes. § 2A-513(1). Additionally, the lessor or supplier may cure within a reasonable time after the original deadline if it reasonably expected the lessee to accept the nonconforming goods with a money allowance. § 2A-513(2).

If the lessee who attempts to reject does not state a defect that is "ascertainable by reasonable inspection," and that defect could have been cured by the lessor, the lessee loses its ability to rely on that defect to justify its rejection or establish default. § 2A-514(1)(a). Moreover, if the lease is between merchants and the lessor after rejection asks in a record [writing] for a statement of defects, any defects not so specified cannot be relied on by the lessee. § 2A-514(1)(b).

The lessee's right to revoke and force the lessor to take the goods back once the lessee has already accepted them is more restricted than the right to reject. It only arises where the nonconformity of the goods substantially impairs their value to the lessee, and either (i) acceptance was made without knowledge of the nonconformity; or (ii) the lessee was unaware of the defect because of the difficulty of discovering it before acceptance; or (iii) the lessee was "induced" to accept the goods without discovering the nonconformity by the lessor's assurances. § 2A-517.

A lessee does have some obligations and rights with respect to rightfully rejected goods. It must hold them for a reasonable time for disposition by the lessor § 2A-509(3)(b) [§ 2A-512(1)(a)], or, if they are perishable and the lessee is a merchant, it may have an obligation to dispose of them itself. § 2A-511(1). Upon rightful rejection or justifiable revocation, the lessee is also empowered to sell the goods, unless the lease agreement provides to the contrary. § 2A-508(4) [(§ 2A-508(5)]. To the extent it may lawfully sell them, the lessee is treated as having a limited "security interest" in the goods. § 2A-508(5).

c. Remedies as to the Goods—Forcing the Lessor to Provide the Goods. In certain circumstances, where the lessor has failed to deliver or has repudiated, the lessee may nonetheless want to enforce the contract and obtain the use of the desired goods. In certain cases, in particular where the goods are unique, or in other proper circumstances, the lessee may compel specific performance of the lease agreement. §§ 2A-508(2)(b), § 2A-521. Additionally, the lessee has the right of replevin or similar rights if the goods have been identified to the contract and the lessee after reasonable effort is unable to effect cover or circumstances demonstrate it could not reasonably obtain cover. § 2A-521(3). In situations where the lessor becomes insolvent within ten days after receipt of the first installment of rent and any security deposit, and the goods are identified and conform to the contract, the lessee may recover the goods as long as it is prepared to perform its rental and security obligations under the lease. § 2A-522.

d. Rights to Recover Damages. When the lessor fails to deliver the goods, or the lessee rightfully rejects or revokes, the lessee has the option of either obtaining replacement goods and suing for damages based upon its "cover" or substitute transaction, or doing without such substituted performance and suing for market damages. § 2A-518(1), 2A-519(1).

Substitute Transactions. Where the lessee in good faith and in a commercially reasonable manner "covers" by leasing substitute goods from a third party under a "lease agreement substantially similar to the original agreement," it is allowed to recover damages based on the cover price. § 2A-518(2). The lessee may recover its actual out-of-pocket costs, based on the difference between the cover price and the rent remaining under the original lease (both reduced to present value) as well as consequential damages. *Id.* Thus, if the original lease of a BMW was for thirty-six months at $500 per month, but upon the lessor's breach the lessee leases an identical vehicle elsewhere, under a substantially similar contract but for $550 per month, then the lessee is entitled to recover the difference between the two amounts. These amounts must be reduced to present value to preclude overcompensation, as discussed below. As a result, the lessee winds up paying $550 per month, but recovers $50 per month from the breaching lessor, and thus acquires the use of the BMW for the contracted amount, $500 per month.

What is a "substantially similar" lease agreement will depend on a number of facts. Not only must the nature of the substitute goods themselves be examined, but in addition the terms of the new lease are important. Factors that may be relevant are "hell or high water" clauses, "net" lease requirements, options to renew or purchase, representations, warranties and covenants of the lessor, the obligations of the lessee (such as obligations to insure), and the services to be provided by the lessor or lessee. § 2A-518, Official Comment 5. There may be times where identical goods are leased, but where merely using the rent under the substitute lease to determine damages would be improper because the parties' obligations under the two leases are drastically different. Thus, a five-year lease of equipment under which the lessor assumes obligations to insure, pay taxes, service, and maintain the equipment may not be substantially similar to a five-year lease of the same equipment under which the lessee assumes those obligations but pays the same amount of rent as under the original lease. To the extent that all of these factors "allocate cost and risk between the lessor and the lessee and thus affect the amount of rent to be paid," they need to be taken into consideration in determining whether the substitute lease is substantially similar to the breached lease. *Id.* As the Official Comments note: "These findings should not be made with scientific precision, as they are a function of economics, nor should they be made independently with respect to the goods and each element of the agreement, as it is important that a sense of commercial judgment pervade the finding." § 2A-518, Official Comment 6.

The comments to the 1987 Official Text noted that the length of the lease term was also a factor that could result in a finding that the lease agreements were not substantially similar. However, the comment to the 1990 Official Text observes that a substitute lease may have a longer term and still be substantially similar "as long as both (a) the lease terms are commercially comparable . . . and (b) the court can fairly apportion a part of the rental payments under the new lease" to the comparable term remaining on the original lease. § 2A-518, Official Comment 7.

In comparing the rents due under the original lease, and the rents due under the substitute lease, the amounts are to be reduced to present value; that is, their present worth rather than future worth is to be determined. § 2A-518(2). Present value is defined in § 2A-103(1)(u) or § 1-201(28) of revised Article 1. One hundred dollars today is not the equivalent of receiving $100 three years from today. In order to take into account the time value of money, under the 1987 Official Text, the rents are discounted to their present value as of the date of the lessor's default under the lease. Unfortunately, however, in most cases there is a gap between the date when the lessor defaults and the date when the lessee is able to arrange a substitute transaction, resulting in under-compensation to the lessee equivalent to the time value of the money during the gap period. Therefore, current Article 2A uses the date of the commencement of the term of the new lease as the appropriate time for making the calculation.

Once the "cover damages" have been determined, the breaching lessor is entitled to a credit for any expenses that the lessee has saved as a result of the lessor's breach. For example, if the lessee would have had to pay transportation costs under the original lease, but does not incur such costs under the substitute lease, these amounts would be "expenses saved." On the other hand, the lessee is entitled to recover both incidental (if, for example, it incurred additional transportation costs) and consequential damages. § 2A-519(1).

Market Damages. When the lessee does not cover, or its cover does not qualify for treatment under § 2A-518, the lessee's damages are based on a hypothetical substitute transaction at "market price": damages are measured by the difference between the present value of the original rent for the remainder of the lease and the present value of the "market rent" for a comparable term. § 2A-519(1). These values are measured as of the date of default. *Id.* The lessee may also recover incidental and consequential damages. § 2A-520. Any expenses saved as a result of the lessor's default are subtracted.

"Market rent" is the amount that the goods subject to the lease contract would bring if leased on identical terms for a period equivalent to the remaining term of the original lease agreement. § 2A-507(1). If such a comparison is unavailable, a reasonable substitute may be used. § 2A-507(2). The lessor and the lessee can also specify the interest rate to be used in the present value calculation, provided such rate is not "manifestly unreasonable." § 1-201(b)(28); § 2A-103(1)(u) and Official Comment (u).

Thus, if a lessee agreed to lease a Windows desktop computer system for three years at $100 per month, even though similar Windows computers normally lease for $120, and the lessor breaches, the lessee is entitled to recover the difference between the two amounts (again reduced to present value), even though it ultimately chooses not to lease a new computer, but instead to purchase one outright.

Damages when the Lessee Retains the Goods. There may be instances where the lessor breaches, as by delivering nonconforming goods or failing to provide agreed services, yet the lessee may decide to retain the goods and sue for damages. In the case of a breach of warranty, if the lessee gives the required notification of nonconformity, the lessee may recover the difference between the value of the leased goods as accepted and the value of the leased goods as warranted, reduced to present value as of the date of acceptance. § 2A-519(4). Again, expenses saved by the lessee need to be deducted, but allowance is made for incidental and consequential damages. § 2A-519(4). So, for example, if the lessee had agreed to lease a Windows computer for $100 per month, but the computer that is delivered is only a 486 machine which normally rents for $80 per month compared to the $120 per month that Windows computers then command, the lessee may recover the difference between the value of the lease if the goods had been delivered as warranted ($120) and the value as accepted ($80), a recovery of $40 per month (reduced to present value, of course). Moreover, the lessee may instead elect to "recover" these sums by exercising its statutory right to offset; upon notice to the lessor, it may deduct the amount of its damages ($40 per month) from the rentals still due under the lease. § 2A-508(6). The result is that the lessee will only be paying $60 per month for the 486 computer, an amount which is $20 per month below the market; this effectively preserves the lessee's benefit of its bargain, for it had originally contracted to obtain a Windows for $20 per month below market.

Where the lessor's breach is other than a breach of warranty, but the lessee opts to keep the goods, it is additionally entitled to recover "the loss resulting in the ordinary course of events from the lessor's default as determined in any manner that is reasonable." § 2A-519(3). Thus, if the lessor fails to perform its obligation to maintain the goods, the lessee may recover any amounts it incurs to get the necessary maintenance, or any amounts naturally flowing from the breach.

e. **Rights to Cancel the Lease Contract.** The lessee is given the right to cancel the lease contract upon the lessor's default. § 2A-508(1)(a). A cancellation by the lessee results in the discharge of all obligations not yet performed by the parties, but does not affect any right based on prior default or performance. § 2A-505(1). Thus, although the cancellation discharges the lessee's obligation to pay rentals accruing after cancellation, the lessee may nonetheless still be liable for any rentals accruing prior to the cancellation. However, the lessee does, despite the cancellation, retain any remedies it may have for default based on the entire lease agreement. § 2A-501(1). In a statutory finance lease, § 2A-103(1)(g) that is not a consumer lease, or a common law "hell or high water" lease, there is no lessee right to cancel the lease, even upon lessor's default. § 2A-517.

C. Lessor's Statutory Rights

1. Lessee Defaults

As is the case with lessors, whether the lessee is in default is determined by (i) the terms of the lease agreement and (ii) Article 2A. § 2A-501(1). A statutory default occurs when the lessee wrongfully rejects or revokes acceptance of the goods, repudiates, or fails to make a payment when due. § 2A-523(1). Thus, it is no longer necessary for a lessor to define nonpayment as a default, but most leases still do so.

Although the rights that flow from a statutory default and a contractual one were theoretically the same under the 1987 Official Text, § 2A-523(1), two problems arose. First, some specific remedy sections were, by their own terms, limited to statutory defaults. Second, and of more concern, objections were raised to allowing recourse to certain statutory remedies (e.g., the right to repossess from the lessee) where the contractual default was minor (e.g., breach of a representation or covenant that caused no loss). Thus, the 1990 Official Text draws a distinction between statutory and contractual defaults, and provides that a contractual default will give rise only to remedies provided in the lease contract or the statutory right to recover for any actual loss incurred, unless the default substantially impairs the value of the lease contract to the lessor. In the case of material contractual defaults (i.e., those substantially impairing the value of the lease contract to the lessor), the lessor has the full panoply of statutory remedies available under Article 2A unless the contract provides otherwise.

a. Statutory Defaults. As noted above, a statutory default occurs where the lessee wrongfully repudiates, rejects, or revokes acceptance, or fails to make a payment when due unless the lease provides otherwise. In these situations, the lessor's remedies are catalogued in § 2A-523(1). They include the options to:

(i)   cancel the lease contract (§ 2A-505(1));

(ii) dispose of, salvage, or complete goods that have not been identified to the lease contract (§ 2A-524);

(iii) withhold delivery of undelivered goods or take possession of delivered goods (§ 2A-525);

(iv) stop delivery of goods by a bailee (§ 2A-526);

(v)   dispose of the goods and recover damages (§ 2A-527), or retain the goods and recover damages (§ 2A-528);

(vi) recover the rent (§ 2A-529); and

(vii) exercise any rights or remedies provided in the lease. § 2A-523(1)(f).

If the lessor does not fully exercise a right or remedy to which it is entitled under § 2A-523(1), it may recover for the loss resulting in the ordinary course of events from the lessee's default as determined in any reasonable manner. § 2A-523(3) [§ 2A-523(2)]. According to the Official Comment, "The intent of the provision is to reject the doctrine of election of remedies and to permit an alteration of course by the lessor unless such alteration would actually have an effect on the lessee that would be unreasonable under the circumstances." § 2A-523, Official Comment 1. Again, the remedies are subject to the general policy that the lessor should be placed in the same position as if performance had occurred, and not in a better position. § 1-305 [§ 1-106].

b. Contractual Defaults. Although not defined in Article 2A, contractual defaults would include any breach designated as a default under the lease agreement, e.g., failure to pay or perform, breaches of representations or covenants. In such a situation, the lessor has all of the rights and remedies provided in the lease contract.

In the event of a contractual default, § 2A-523 specifically gives the lessor the following remedies: (i) if the default substantially impairs the value of the lease contract to the lessor (i.e., if it is a material default, as opposed to a technical default), the lessor is given all the rights given to lessors in the event of a statutory default; but (ii) if the default does not substantially impair the value of the lease contract (i.e., it is immaterial), the lessor may only recover under § 2A-523(2) the loss resulting in the ordinary course of events from the lessee's default as determined in any reasonable manner. § 2A-523(3). The contract may, of course, set out how those losses are to be measured, subject to the restrictions placed on liquidated damages clauses and also to the rule that the obligations of reasonableness may not be disclaimed. § 1-302 (b) [§ 1-201(3)].

2. LESSOR REMEDIES

a. In General. As previously described, when the lessee is in default, the lessor has a range of remedies. These remedies can be categorized as (i) remedies regarding the goods; (ii) remedies for damages; and (iii) remedies regarding the lease contract. As discussed later, some remedies arise under different circumstances.

b. Remedies as to the Goods. When a lessee in possession of leased goods is in default, the lessor may repossess the goods whether or not the lease contains a repossession right. § 2A-525(2).

This is an important provision that recognizes and protects the lessor's residual rights in the goods, and is a right drawn from Article 9 on Secured Transactions. The right to proceed to repossess without judicial process, i.e., the right to self-help repossession, is available only if it can be accomplished without breach of the peace. § 2A-525(3). Case law under the comparable provision in § 9-609 will undoubtedly be used to determine what constitutes a breach of the peace.

Once the lessor has repossessed the goods, there is no such provision such as is present in Article 9 on Secured Transactions permitting the lessee to redeem the goods by paying the amount due and owing; this type of provision, while appropriate to protect the lessee's equity in collateral subject to a security interest, is inappropriate where the lessor retains a residual interest in the goods. Thus, the court in *In re Lamar*, 249 B.R. 822 (Bankr. S.D. Ga. 2000) held that a lessee does not have the right to redeem or recover repossessed property unless it is specifically granted in the lease.

In addition to the right to repossess, the lessor may withhold delivery of undelivered goods, or stop delivery of goods by a bailee. § 2A-525, 2A-526. Whether repossessing or stopping delivery, the lessor may proceed to dispose of the goods by re-letting to a new party, sale, or otherwise. § 2A-527(1).

Even absent a breach by the lessee, if the lessor discovers that the lessee is insolvent, it may refuse to deliver the goods. § 2A-525(l).

c. Remedies for Damages. As with the lessee's remedies, the lessor's remedies hinge on (i) whether it enters into a substitute transaction and re-leases the goods; (ii) whether it retains the goods; or (iii) whether the lessee remains in possession.

Substitute Transaction. The lessor under Article 2A who either retains or repossesses the goods may proceed to dispose of the goods through sale, lease, or other disposition. The amounts received by the lessor under that substitute transaction may be taken into account in determining damages only if the disposition is (i) by a lease agreement substantially similar to the original lease agreement; (ii) made in good faith; and (iii) made in a commercially reasonable manner. § 2A-527(2).

The factors to be considered in determining whether the substitute lease is "substantially similar" to the original lease include options to purchase or re-lease; the lessor's representations, warranties, and covenants to the lessee and those of the lessee to the lessor; and the services, if any, to be provided by each party. § 2A-527, Official Comments. If all these factors taken into account demonstrate that the two leases are substantially similar, then the rentals under the substitute lease are used in calculating the lessor's damages. *Id.*

There may be instances where there are substantial differences between the obligations assumed by each party, but the value of those differences can be calculated. If the differences between the two leases can be easily valued, the court may adjust the difference in rent between the two leases by taking into account the different provisions, and still award damages based on the substitute contract. *Id.* A hypothetical posed in the Official Comment to Section 2A-527 illustrates the difference in approach:

> Assume that A buys a jumbo tractor for $1 million and then leases the tractor to B for a term of thirty-six months. The tractor is delivered to and is accepted by B on May 1. On June 1, B fails to pay the monthly rent to A. B returns the tractor to A, who immediately re-leases the tractor to C for a term identical to the term remaining under the lease between A and B. All terms and conditions under the lease between A and C are identical to those under the original lease between A and B, except that C does not provide any property damage or other insurance coverage, and B agrees to provide complete coverage. Coverage is expensive and difficult to obtain. § 2A-527, Official Comment 6.

If it is possible to adjust the recovery to take account of the difference between the two leases, the substitute damages provisions can be used. *Id.* Thus, if the substitute lease requires the lessor to insure the equipment, and the lessor can establish that coverage would cost $10,000, then it should be allowed to recover the present value of the difference in rentals between the two leases and an additional $10,000 to compensate for the difference between the insurance provisions in the leases. *Id.*

If the disposition for any reason does not qualify under § 2A-527(2), or the disposition is by sale or otherwise, then the situation is treated as if the lessor chose not to dispose of the goods, and damages are measured under § 2A-528. § 2A-527(3).

Substitute Transaction Calculations. When the lessor has entered into a substantially similar lease transaction, the lessor's damages consist of the following:

   (i)   the accrued and unpaid rent;

   (ii) the difference between the total rent for the remaining term of the original lease and the total rent for the lease term of the lease to the new lessee, reduced to present value; and

   (iii) incidental damages minus expenses saved.

The amount of accrued and unpaid rent is determined as of the date of commencement of the new lease, recognizing that between the time of default and the time when the new lessee becomes responsible, the lessor is entitled to some type of recovery. The amount of rentals under the remaining term is determined as of the date of commencement of the new lease as well.

A simple hypothetical illustrates the operation of this section. Assume on January 1, 2007, lessor leases a tractor to lessee for thirty-six months at $1,000 per month. Lessee pays rent for six months, then defaults, whereupon on September 1 the lessor repossesses. It is able to arrange a new lease of the tractor beginning on January 1, 2008, for a twenty-four-month period at $800 per month. The lessor would be able to recover for six months of accrued, unpaid rentals covering the period from lessee's default until the beginning of the new lease term. In addition, it would be able to recover the total rentals remaining on the original lease ($24,000) minus the rentals due on the substitute lease ($19,200), reduced to present value.

Market Damages. If the lessor does not re-lease the goods, or if its disposition for any reason does not qualify under § 2A-527(2), damages are measured under a "market rent" formula set forth in § 2A-528(1). Under this section, the lessor may recover as damages:

(i) accrued and unpaid rentals as of the time of default (or, under the 1990 text, if the lessee has taken possession, as of the time of repossession by the lessor or re-tender by the lessee);

(ii) the difference between the total rent for the remaining term of the original lease, and the market rent for the same lease term, reduced to present value (measured by the time of default, time of repossession, or time of re-tender, as above); and

(iii) incidental expenses minus expenses saved.

As in the case of lessee's remedies, "market rent" is the amount which the goods subject to the lease contract would bring if leased on identical terms for a period identical to the remaining term of the original lease agreement. § 2A-507(1). Thus, assume the lessee defaults when there are fourteen months remaining on the lease of a computer system for $200 a month. The lessor repossesses the goods, but does not re-lease them for two months even though, had it done so, the lessor could have commanded $150 a month in rentals. The lessor could recover all unpaid rentals up until the time of repossession ($400). In addition, it could recover acceler-ated future rentals for the remainder of the lease term (12 months x $200/month) minus the market rent for the same lease term (12 months x $150/month), or a sum of $50 a month for twelve months, reduced to present value. In effect, the deduction for the market rent operates to impose an obligation on the lessor to mitigate its damages and re-lease the goods by denying recovery to the extent it fails to do so.

"Lost-Profits" Damages. Whenever the above "market damage" formula is inadequate to place the lessor in as good a position as if performance had occurred, the lessor may recover under § 2A-528(2) for its lost profits, including reasonable overhead. This section would operate to protect "lost-volume" lessors and would protect the lessor in the following situation. Assume a dealer has a fleet of Ford sedans, virtually identical in all respects other than color. Lessee A, who has contracted to lease a blue sedan for three years, breaches the lease. A second potential Lessee B, who also wants to lease a Ford sedan, decides that instead of the green car he wanted originally, he would take the available blue car. In such an instance, the lessor could demonstrate that, had Lessee A not breached, it would have been able to lease both the blue sedan (to Lessee A) and the green sedan (to Lessee B). Thus, it should be entitled to recover its lost profits on the lease to Lessee A, even though it could and did lease the blue sedan to Lessee B at the same lease price. This amount of profit is reduced to present value.

There is a second situation where lost profit recovery may be appropriate even though it is theoretically possible to use a substitute transaction or market damage formula. Assume a lessee repudiates a finance lease prior to delivery or acceptance of the goods. Theoretically, the lessor could nonetheless complete its purchase of the goods under the supply contract, and then lease them under a substitute finance lease; if the market rental were equal to that under the original lease contract, then the lessor would suffer no loss using either a substitute transaction formula or a market damages formula. If, however, the lessor were to cancel the supply contract because a substitute lease was not likely to be possible, it should be entitled to its lost profits under § 2A-528(2). If it had already acquired the goods, it could dispose of them by sale; in that case, the lessor could still recover its lost profits, as well as its cost of acquiring the goods, but would have to give a credit for the proceeds of disposition.

Action for the Rent. The lessor may have an action for the rent due under the lease, § 2A-529, in the event of a contractual default that substantially impairs the value of the lease agreement. See § 2A-523(3).

An action for rent is available in the following three circumstances:

(i)   the goods had been accepted by the lessee and not repossessed or re-tendered;

(ii) the goods were lost or destroyed within a commercially reasonable time after risk of loss passed to the lessee; or

(iii) the lessor was unable to dispose of identified goods after reasonable efforts at a reasonable price, or circumstances indicate such an effort would be unavailing. In these instances, the lessee has either received what it bargained for, assumed the risk of loss of the goods, or there is no "market" through which a damages calculation may be made.

Article 2A gives an action for the price of accepted goods only where the goods have not been re-tendered or repossessed. Therefore, if the breaching lessee in possession of goods tells the lessor to "come and get them," the lessor cannot ignore that request and expect to hold the lessee liable for the full rentals due. In such cases, the lessor may only recover the price if it is unable to sell the leased goods; otherwise, the lessor is relegated to its re-lease and market damages.

When the lessor is entitled to receive the price, it is entitled to:

(i)   accrued and unpaid rent;

(ii) the present value of the rent for the remaining lease term; and

(iii) incidental expenses minus expenses saved. § 2A-529(1)(a)-(b).

The accrued rent and present value of future rents are determined as of the date of the entry of the judgment. *Id.*

d. Remedies as to the Lease Contract. The lessor is given the right to cancel the lease contract upon the lessee's default. § 2A-523(1)(a). A cancellation by the lessor results in the discharge of all obligations not yet performed by the parties, but does not affect any right based on prior default or performance. Thus, although the cancellation discharges the lessee's contractual obligation to keep the leased property insured, the lessee may nonetheless still be liable for any result flowing from its failure to maintain insurance prior to cancellation. The lessor does, despite the cancellation, retain any remedies it may have for default based on the entire lease agreement. § 2A-501(4). The lessor can also still recover full damages for infringement of a right occurring before cancellation.

CHAPTER

9

THIRD-PARTY RIGHTS

In modern commerce, leases do not exist in a universe confined to the lessor, lessee, and supplier of the goods. Third parties may be affected by a lease transaction, whether their status is as a financer, buyer, sublessee, real estate claimant, etc. Lessors often use (and may need) third-party financing, using the lease and the goods as collateral; for many lessors, this is the only way they can acquire the goods. To a lesser extent, some lessees may wish to obtain credit by pledging their leasehold interest as collateral. Both lessors and lessees may find that their respective circumstances have changed since inception of the lease, and may need to transfer their rights in the goods or the lease to a third party. In any case, the leased goods may constitute fixtures or accessions under applicable non-Code law, giving rise to claims to the goods by real estate claimants.

Article 2A furnishes several helpful principles governing the rights of lessor and lessee in each of these circumstances, where third-party rights are also implicated. The three main principles that recur throughout the area are these. First, the interest of the parties should be freely alienable or transferable. Second, if the transfer is detrimental to the nontransferring party (i.e., it "materially impairs the risk of obtaining return performance") the nontransferring party is entitled to damages or other appropriate relief. Third, contractual prohibitions against transfer do not affect the validity of the transfer, although they may give rise to damages against the transferor or other appropriate relief.

Of course, it is important at the outset wherever third parties are involved to define what property interest the third party is claiming and the nature of its claim. The third party, for example, may claim the lessor's or the lessee's entire interest under the lease contract, claiming that it is a transferee. Section A below discusses transferees of the lease contract, including discussion of transfers of rights under the lease contract (e.g., transfer of the right to receive rentals under the lease contract). Alternatively, the third party may claim the goods themselves, claiming that it is a transferee of the goods from either the lessor or the lessee. Section B below discusses the rights of alleged transferees of the goods themselves.

A special kind of third party—the creditor—who makes its claim to either the goods or the lease contract as a result of its relationship with either the lessor or lessee is discussed in section C. A special note: as will be discussed, an important third-party claim is the claim of a secured party to a security interest in the goods, the leasehold, or the lessor's residual interest. Comprehensive treatment of the rights to secured parties thus requires reference to Revised Article 9, especially § 9-407.

A. Transferees of the Lease Contract

When a lease contract is entered into, both the lessor and lessee have valuable rights under that lease. The lessor's interest includes, among other things, the right to receive a stream of rental income during the period of the lease. The lessee's interest is the right to use and possess the goods for the lease term. In each case, these interests are valuable rights that the parties may choose to transfer.

Many leases are entered into with the expectation that the lessor will transfer its interest in the lease (and potentially the leased goods themselves) to another lessor, whether through outright sale or by a transfer intended for collateral purposes. (Grants or foreclosure of security interests will be addressed in section C). Smaller leasing companies, for example, usually have limited capital to invest in goods that they in turn lease out. As a result, these smaller companies cannot wait until rentals are fully paid under an executed lease to reinvest the money. Consequently, these smaller companies frequently sell the leases that they have originated to another lessor, at a marked-up price reflecting the original lessee's fees for its origination services. The purchasing lessor benefits from this transaction because it does not have to employ a marketing staff to originate the leases. If its cost of capital is lower than that of the smaller company, its investment in such acquired leases can be profitable, even at a marked-up acquisition price.

Although these kinds of outright lessor transfers usually occur before or shortly after delivery of the leased equipment, there may be reasons for a lessor to transfer leases at other times. The original lessor may lose access to advantageous financing, or may need to sell one or more leases and the related equipment in order to raise capital. A lessor may decide to exit the leasing business if such operations are no longer sufficiently profitable. Changes in the law (such as tax law or bank capital requirements) also may render less attractive its investment in leases and associated equipment. For these reasons, the lessor needs the flexibility under the lease to sell or pledge its interest in the contract and the equipment.

Similarly, there also are many reasons why a lessee will want to transfer its interest in a lease. A merger or other corporate combination may eliminate the initial lessee and require transfer of the lease. The lessee may change its line of business from that for which the leased equipment was necessary. Or the lessee may simply need to reduce its cost of long-term assets.

Article 2A's general approach is that both the lessor's and the lessee's leasehold interests should be freely transferable. The primary limitation, designed to protect the interests of the nontransferring party, arises where the transfer materially increases the burdens or risks placed upon the nontransferring party. § 2A-303(4)(b). Both voluntary and involuntary transfers of either the lessee's or lessor's leasehold interest are effective, notwithstanding a prohibition in the lease or a lease provision making such a transfer an event of default. § 2A-303(2). Contractual prohibitions on transfers do not automatically void any attempted transfer, although, as noted below, they may give rise to other rights § 2A-303(2).

Under Article 2A, however, neither party has an unfettered right to transfer. If the transfer constitutes an event of default under the lease, then the aggrieved party ("unless that party waives the default or otherwise agrees") may exercise all of its rights and remedies under Article 2A as well as its rights and remedies under the lease itself (except where Article 2A otherwise would prohibit enforcement of such lease provisions). § 2A-303(4)(a). If the lease contract does not make the transfer an event of default, but such transfer either is prohibited by the lease or "materially impairs the prospect of obtaining return performance by, materially changes the duty of, or materially increases the burden or risk imposed upon" the nontransferring party (hereinafter called a "Materially Adverse Transfer"), then the nontransferring party, "unless (it) agrees at any time to the transfer in the lease contract or otherwise," may recover damages "caused by the transfer to the extent that the damages could not reasonably be prevented" by the aggrieved party and may obtain "other appropriate relief, including cancellation of the lease contract or an injunction against the transfer." § 2A-303(4)(b).

For instance, if a lessor induces the lessee to enter into the lease by citing its maintenance capabilities, then a transfer of the lease to a mere financing lessor, or a lessor far less qualified to service the goods, would seem to be a Materially Adverse Transfer. The transfer to the financing lessor would not be ineffective, but the lessee would have rights against the lessor under § 2A-303(4)(b). Similarly, if a proprietary hospital known for its well-to-do patients were to transfer its leasehold interest as lessee to another health care facility which was dependent upon less reliable funding, then arguably "the burden or risk" of nonpayment has been materially increased upon the lessor, who deserves relief under § 2A-303(4)(b).

Most leases usually limit the lessee's ability to transfer, in any way, all or any portion of its rights under the lease agreement. The theory is that the lessor and any related financing participant have bargained for the credit and character of the original lessee to pay rent and perform its other lease obligations. Even though it is likely that a large commercial lessee will have the right to sublet or assign its leasehold interest, the lessee in such case usually remains fully responsible for all of its obligations under the lease. It is most unusual (but not unprecedented), however, for the lease contract to restrict transfer of the lessor's leasehold interest.

Article 2A severely limits contractual restraints on transfer. The first such limitation involves transfers of monetary rights. Although the transfer of the lease by one of the parties may cause the other party to feel insecure about whether future performance will be forthcoming, there is no such problem when all that is being transferred is a monetary right, e.g., a right to damages or right to payment. As a result, restraints on any transfer of a right to damages for default or on the right to payment or rentals under the lease are not enforceable, and any such transfer is not a Materially Adverse Transfer. § 2A-303(3). Official Comment 3 to § 2A-303 dispels any doubt whether a lessor can transfer the right to future payments under the lease. The mere fact that the lessor is obligated to allow the lessee to remain in possession and to use the goods as long as the lessee is not in default does not mean that there is "remaining performance" on the part of the lessor.

A second limitation on contractual restraints concerns lessees who transfer their leasehold interests despite a contractual prohibition thereto. Although Article 2A does not declare such restraints unenforceable, as it does in the case of monetary rights, it does limit the effect of such restraints. It first provides that any transfers in violation of the contractual restraint are nonetheless effective. § 2A-303(2). Assume that, despite a contractual prohibition on transfer, the lessee nonetheless transfers its leasehold interest. The transfer itself is effective, but if the lease agreement makes the transfer an event of default, then although the assignee acquires rights under the assignment of the lease, the lease itself has been breached, giving the lessor the rights to remedies for breach under § 2A-501(2). § 2A-303(4)(a).

If, however, the prohibited transfer is not made an event of default, the nontransferring party has the right to seek judicial relief, including cancellation of the lease contract or an injunction against the transfer. § 2A-303(4)(b). In this connection, the comments to § 2A-303 helpfully observe that "if a transfer gives rise to the rights and remedies provided in subsection (4), the transferee . . . may propose, and the other party may accept, adequate cure or compensation for past defaults and adequate assurance of future due performance ... subsection (4) does not preclude any other relief that may be available to [the aggrieved party], such as an action for interference with contractual relations." § 2A-303, Official Comment 7.

Article 9 in § 9-407 addresses a third limitation on contractual restraints on transfer, which will be discussed in greater detail in section C.1, below. Specifically, § 9-407 provides that a lease provision making the creation or enforcement of a security interest in the lessor's interest an event of default is not enforceable by the lessee, except where enforcement actually results in a delegation of material performance of the lessor. § 9-407(c).

Therefore §§ 2A-303 and 9-407 together validate prohibited transfers, although an impermissible transferee from the lessee may have to deal with a lease that is in default. However, § 9-407(b) renders such prohibitions effective "to the extent there is (1) a transfer by the lessee of the lessee's right of possession and use of the goods in violation of the [applicable lease] term or (2) a delegation of a material performance" of the lessee in violation of the applicable lease covenant. § 9-407(b)(1), (2). In effect, just as the lessee can protect itself against transfers by the lessor of material obligations for which the lessee has bargained, so can the lessor restrain (and perhaps block) actual delegation of material performance by the lessee whether through an outright transfer, or indirectly through a leasehold mortgage.

One final note: in a consumer lease, any prohibition on transfer of either party's leasehold interest, and any provision making such a transfer an event of default, "must be specific, by a writing, and conspicuous." § 2A-303(7).

B. Transferees of the Goods

A true lease is a significantly different transaction than a sale of goods (under Article 2) or a secured financing (under Article 9). In the latter two instances, the person owing the payment obligation is the owner of the goods, but in a true lease, the party responsible for payment of the rentals is a mere bailee of the goods. By contrast, the lessor of the goods is and remains the owner. All the lease does is hand a temporary right to use and control goods to the lessee. Section 2A-103(1)(q) recognizes the "lessor's residual interest" as the lessor's continuing rights in the goods, including the right to reacquire them upon termination of the lease. The lessor's residual interest does not depend on the existence of the lease agreement and is separate from the respective "leasehold interest" of the lessor and the lessee. The residual interest needs to be protected. The third-party transfer rules of Article 2A protect that residual interest in two ways. First, the lessor's ability to transfer its interest in the goods is protected. Second, the ability of the lessee to transfer an interest in the goods (as opposed to the lease itself) is sharply curtailed.

1. TRANSFERS OF THE LESSOR'S INTEREST IN THE GOODS

Here again the basic rule is that the lessor may transfer its residual interest in goods (including creating a security interest) notwithstanding a lease provision purporting to prohibit transfer of the lessor's residual or make such a transfer an event of default. § 2A-303(2) and Comment 1. Although such a prohibited transfer will give rise to certain remedies, it nonetheless will be "otherwise effective." § 2A-303(2).

Moreover, if the transfer is the grant of a security interest in the lessor's residual, under the general rules of § 2A-303, the transfer in no way impairs the lessee's expectation of the lessor's performance under the lease contract. Hence, the grant of a security interest will never be a Materially Adverse Transfer. § 9-407(c). A grant of a security interest in the lessor's residual gives rise to remedies if and only if there is "a delegation of a material performance of [the lessor] in violation of the [applicable lease] term." § 9-407(b). Since it is implausible that a secured lender, taking as collateral the lessor's residual interest in the goods, would accept any delegation to it of a material obligation of the lessor under the lease, it is likely that § 9-407 validates most conventional borrowing arrangements by lessors using the goods as collateral. Contractual restraints on the lessor's transfer of its residual interest will be discussed more fully in section C.2, below.

The purchaser of the goods may also acquire the accompanying lease of those goods. So long as the original lessor retains the obligation to perform any material duties under the lease, such as maintaining and servicing the equipment or providing upgrades of the equipment on a periodic basis in order to avoid obsolescence, such a transfer of the lease should be valid. § 2A-303, Official Comment 3. Usually, where the lease places such duties on the lessor, the original lessor either will retain any material lessor obligations, or will include a lease provision whereby the lessee consents to any future sale of the goods, assignment of the lease, and substitution of the transferee as the party responsible for the lessor's obligations under the lease. Retention of material lessor obligations is the likely scenario in a so-called "wraparound" lease of equipment, under which the original lessor sells the equipment to a third party and leases it back, remaining as the lessor under the original lease and hence obligated to the lessee as if the sale-leaseback never occurred. On the other hand, substitution of the new equipment owner as the party responsible for the lessor obligations is typical in portfolio sales where the original lessor may be trying to reduce its involvement in a particular kind of equipment or industry group.

Increasingly, a pool of hundreds or thousands of leases is "securitized," i.e., the lessor transfers them to a bankruptcy-remote company, usually a wholly owned subsidiary. In most cases, these leases are "net" leases and contain no material lessor obligations, but if there are such duties, then the lessor in the securitization contracts is appointed as servicer of the leases and agrees to discharge the lessor duties. That way, the lessee cannot claim that a Materially Adverse Transfer has occurred or that it is insecure.

In another case, a lessor may want to enter into a subsequent lease to begin upon expiration of the prior lease. For example, a lessor may lease goods to Lessee A for the first 40 percent of the goods' economic life. Before the term of that lease has expired, the lessor may contract to lease the same goods to Lessee B for all or any part of the remaining economic life of the goods, commencing on a date on or subsequent to expiration of the first lease. Under such a subsequent lease of the goods, the subsequent lessee obtains, to the extent bargained for in the subsequent lease, whatever leasehold interest "the lessor had or had power to transfer" and "takes subject to the existing lease contract." § 2A-304 and Official Comment 4.

There are two situations where the subsequent lessee takes free of the existing lease. The first is where the subsequent lessee leases in the ordinary course of business from a merchant who has been entrusted with the goods by the existing lessee. § 2A-304(2). For example, suppose a lessee entrusts the leased goods to the lessor for refurbishment. A subsequent lessee who leases the entrusted goods from that entrustee lessor in the ordinary course of business takes free of the existing, prior lease contract. Alternatively, if the subsequent lessee leases in good faith, for value and as part of a post-default disposition of the goods by the lessor under § 2A-527, it will take free of the existing lease. If Lessee A defaults and the lessor disposes of the goods (without first canceling Lease A) by leasing them to Lessee B in good faith and for value, then Lessee B takes free of Lessee A's rights. Even though the volume of subsequent lease transactions does not appear to be substantial, Article 2A has performed a service by clarifying the rights of subsequent lessees.

2. Transfers of the Lessee's Interest in the Goods

The general rule is that the lessee has no right to transfer any interest in the goods, as opposed to in the lease itself. This general rule recognizes the fact that the lessor is the owner of the residual interest in the goods, and that any attempt by the lessee to transfer the goods (as opposed to the lease) potentially interferes with that residual interest.

There are, however, two exceptions to the general rule. The first arises when the lessee is a merchant dealing in goods of the kind. In order to protect the marketplace, Article 2A provides that such a lessee may pass good title to a buyer in the ordinary course of business or to a lessee in the ordinary course of business. § 2A-305(2). The transferee (whether buyer or lessee) obtains, to the extent of the interest transferred, all of the lessor's and the lessee's interest in the goods, and takes free of the existing lease contract. This exception parallels the rule found in other parts of the Code, and particularly in § 2-402, which attempts to protect buyers in the ordinary course by placing the risk on the owner of goods who entrusts them to a merchant.

In *Mercedes-Benz Credit Corp. v. Johnson*, 110 Cal.App.4th 53 (2003), the lessee, a used car dealer, sold the car that he had leased for his personal use from Mercedes-Benz. The buyer of the car claimed that he had superior title to the car as against Mercedes-Benz Credit Corp. because he was a buyer in the ordinary course of business and the seller was a dealer in automobiles. The court, relying on California's nonuniform version of the definition of "entrustment," which limits protection of buyers in the ordinary course of business to situations where the goods were entrusted to a merchant for the purpose of sale, obtaining offers to purchase, locating a buyer, or the like, found that there had been no entrustment in this case and that therefore the lessor's interest in the goods was superior to that of the buyer. The result may well have been different if the uniform version of Article 2A had applied.

The second exception to the general rule recognizes that, in certain narrow situations, the lessee's interest may arise prior to the lease, such as in a sale-leaseback transaction. In a sale-leaseback transaction, A sells a good to B and then leases that good back from B. Thus, A had an interest in the good before the lease arose. Section 2A-308(3) helpfully provides that "retention of possession of the goods pursuant to a lease contract entered into by the seller as lessee and the buyer as lessor in connection with the sale or identification of the goods is not fraudulent if the buyer bought for value and in good faith." The Official Comment notes that section 2A-308 "states a new rule with respect to sale-leaseback transactions" and is expected to avoid the unintended effort, delay, and uncertainty caused by "vendor in possession" or other fraudulent conveyance statutes in many states. Section 2A-308(3) thus will be a substantial benefit not only to lessors in wraparound structures, but also to lessees wishing to use lease financing for equipment already in use on their premises. Strictly speaking, however, a wraparound lease or a sale-leaseback is not so much a transfer of the lessee's interest in the goods as it is a transfer of the goods by someone who simultaneously becomes a lessee.

C. Creditors

1. CREDITORS WITH A SECURITY INTEREST IN THE LEASE

a. Lessor's Creditors. The policy of free transferability found in Article 2A and Article 9 also applies in favor of creditors whose loan is collateralized by a security interest in the lease. Thus, even if the grant or enforcement of a security interest in the lease constitutes a breach of the lease, the grant or enforcement of the security interest nonetheless will be effective. § 9-407(a). As mentioned in section A above, subsection (a) provides that a restriction in a lease on creation or enforcement of a security interest in the lessor's leasehold interest is not enforceable at all unless there is a "delegation of a material performance" which violates that lease restriction. § 9-407(b)(2). Freedom of alienability is essential if lessors and owners of goods are to conduct transactions that maximize the value of their property, as evidenced by the substantial number of personal property leases that serve as collateral for loans to the lessor.

Section 9-407 addresses attempted restraints on the creation or enforcement of a security interest in the lessor's leasehold interest. This section along with § 2A-303(2) recognizes the lessor's traditional rights to pledge the lease, much like § 9-406(d) prevents account debtors from blocking sales or other assignments of their accounts. The theory is that generally the lessor's interest under a lease and its right to the rental stream is an asset that the lessor should have available to sell or pledge as collateral. Consequently, a lease provision prohibiting the creation or enforcement of a security interest in the lessor's interest under the lease contract, or making such a transfer an event of default, is not enforceable by the lessee. § 9-407(a).

The only exception arises when the lessor's duties under the lease that are material in nature are also delegated. § 9-407(b)(2), (c). This exception reflects the Article 2 policy protecting parties to a sale contract from delegation of a material performance obligation that may adversely affect the interests of the other party. § 2-210(2). The general rule, however, is that the creation or enforcement of a security interest in the lessor's leasehold interest does not adversely affect the lessee and hence is not a Materially Adverse Transfer. § 9-407(c). There are two potentially troubling situations, however, which creditors claiming a security interest in the lease may encounter. The first occurs when the security interest arises from the sale of the lease (as opposed to being merely given as security). To the extent that the sale of the lease results in a delegation of duties to the secured creditor/purchaser, the transfer might well qualify as a Materially Adverse Transfer. The second situation occurs when the secured creditor forecloses upon its security interest in the lease and the transfer constitutes such a delegation of lessor duties as to be a Materially Adverse Transfer.

Lessors who anticipate assigning or transferring their leasehold or residual interests and want to avoid issues as to whether such actions are "material delegations" may wish to include lease provisions specifically permitting the lessor to transfer its interest without activating any of the lessee's Article 2A remedies. This is particularly important in light of the lessee's right under § 2A-401 to claim insecurity as to the lessor's future performance and to suspend its performance until it receives adequate assurance from the lessor as to performance of the lessor's duties.

Many leases are known as "net leases," under which the lessee is responsible for maintaining, insuring, returning, etc. the goods, and the lessor's sole responsibility is not to violate the lessee's quiet enjoyment rights to the leased goods. With such leases, if the lessor uses the lease as collateral for a loan or transfers the lease outright, there should be little concern over the "actual delegation" scenario, because there is no "material performance" to delegate. Good practice nonetheless suggests that any such lease stipulate that any transfer of the lessor's leasehold interest would not constitute a Materially Adverse Transfer. This makes sense because such a lessor essentially furnishes financing rather than a short-term bailment of the goods. In return for ceding such freedom to the lessor, many lease transactions provide for the lessor and any transferee to covenant that they will respect the lessee's quiet enjoyment rights, so long as the lessee does not default under the lease and the transferee continues to receive all rent payable under the lease. (See Chapter 7.A for an example of such a clause.)

Of course, there may be other transfers of the lessor's leasehold interest that are in the nature of a security transfer but are not sales of or the grant of a security interest in the entire leasehold interest. For instance, simply the rental stream under the lease may be sold. In practice there are any number of creative "rent strip" structures in which the "rent" is "stripped" from the lease and sold. The lessor, for example, may be securitizing a large number of leases, under which the rentals may be sold while the lessor or a transferor retains ownership of the leased equipment. Article 2A accommodates these developments in financial structuring.

For the reasons outlined above, any prohibition on transfer "of a right to payment arising out of the transferor's due performance of the transferor's entire obligation," or any attempt to make such a transfer an event of default, are unenforceable and do not constitute a Materially Adverse Transfer triggering remedies under § 2A-303. § 2A-303(3). However, the Official Comments to § 2A-303 remind us that, in the unlikely event that a transfer by the lessor of its mere right to payment due under the lease gives the lessee reasonable grounds for insecurity of the lessor's ability to perform in the future, then the lessee may exercise its rights to demand adequate assurance of future performance under § 2A-401. § 2A-303, Official Comment 7. So it is advisable for the lease contract to waive the § 2A-401 rights if the lease will be part of any exotic financing arrangement.

b. Lessee's Creditors. In keeping with the Article 2A policy of treating lessors and lessees alike, any prohibition upon, or event of default arising from, the creation or enforcement of a security interest in the lessee's leasehold interest (such as a leasehold mortgage) is unenforceable. § 9-407(a). An exception exists to the extent that there is "...an actual transfer by the lessee of the lessee's right to possession or use of the goods in violation of" the lease restriction. § 9-407(b)(1). Moreover, even though an enforceable event of default may arise upon such an actual transfer if the lease contract so provides, the leasehold mortgagee has the right to offer to cure such breach, compensate the lessor for past defaults, and assure the lessor of the mortgagee's due future performance of the lessee's obligations. § 2A-303, Official Comment 7.

So if the lessee has a valuable lease (perhaps because the rent is now less than fair market value, or the equipment is in short supply), the lease could constitute valuable collateral. If the leasehold mortgagee (i.e., the lessee's creditor) were to foreclose, if such foreclosure were an event of default under the lease, and if the lessor could then cancel the lease contract and repossess the goods, the lessee and the leasehold mortgage would forfeit a valuable lease. To guard against such a forfeiture, the leasehold mortgagee may offer to cure such defaults, give adequate assurances of future performance, and effectively reinstate the lease. This in turn benefits the lessor which might accept a financially viable mortgagee's offer (to cure all defaults and assure lessor of future performance), rather than take a chance on recovering its losses from a defaulting lessee and remarketing the equipment to an as-yet unidentified purchaser or new lessee.

2. CREDITORS WITH A SECURITY INTEREST IN THE GOODS

The now familiar general rule of §§ 2A-303(2) and 9-407 also applies to transactions involving the grant of a security interest in the goods: even if the grant or enforcement of a security interest in the goods constitutes a breach of the lease, the grant or enforcement of such security interest nonetheless will be effective, although the lessor still may be deemed in default. Such a lease restriction is not enforceable unless the grant or enforcement of the security interest results in "an actual delegation of a material performance" that violates the lease provision. § 9-407(a)(b).

Article 2A and Article 9 recognize that the lessor needs the freedom to encumber its residual interest in the goods, not only as a general right attendant to ownership of property but also as an essential means for many lessors to finance their acquisition of the equipment. Article 2A permits enforcement of lessee restraints on such lessor rights only if the lessee arguably would suffer by "actual delegation of a material [lessor] performance," so a lessee cannot attempt to cancel the lease and evade its responsibilities just because there is a grant or foreclosure of a security interest in the leased property without any ensuing harm to the lessee. Consequently, it is likely that in net leases (containing few if any lessor obligations), restraints on granting or enforcing security interests in the goods will be unenforceable.

a. Lessor's Creditors. As noted earlier, a lessor may grant a security interest in the goods to a secured creditor, despite any contractual restriction in the lease and without any fear that such a grant will be deemed a Materially Adverse Transfer. Moreover, there are instances where the lessor may have granted a security interest in the goods prior to the execution of the lease agreement. In the absence of any default by the lessor in its obligations to the secured party, the mere grant of such a security interest will not interfere with the lessee's right to use and possess the goods under the lease. § 2A-307.

If the lessor defaults in its obligations to the secured party, however, and the secured party wants to repossess the goods subject to the lease, it comes into direct conflict with the lessee's claim to the goods under the lease. The general rule is that a creditor of the lessor (including the secured party) takes subject to the lease agreement. § 2A-307(2). Hence, the secured party may not repossess the goods absent a default by the lessee under the lease agreement.

The only exception to this general rule in Article 2A arises where the secured party holds a security interest that attached under Article 9 before the lease contract became enforceable. § 2A-307(2)(c). Even if the security interest attached first, however, the lessee may still be able to take free of the security interest if one of three provisions in Article 9 applies. First, if the lessee gives value and takes delivery of the goods before the security interest is perfected, the lessee will take free of the security interest. § 9-317(c). This is consistent with the other rules in Article 9 that subordinate an unperfected security interest to subsequent transferees. Second, if the lessee is a lessee in the ordinary course of business, the lessee will take free of the security interest whether or not it is perfected. § 9-321(c). Third, the lessee will take free of a security interest to the extent that it secured future advances made either forty-five days after the lease contract becomes enforceable or after the secured party acquires knowledge of the security interest, whichever comes first. § 9-323(f).

Assume, for example, the secured party takes a security interest in the debtor's combine, and takes all steps to perfect its security interest. Subsequently, the debtor leases the combine to the lessee. Although the general rule is that the creditor of the lessor takes subject to the lease contract, here the perfected security interest predated the lease agreement, so the lessee takes subject to that security interest. If, however, the debtor-lessor was in the business of selling and leasing combines, and the lessee was a lessee in the ordinary course of business, the lessee would take free and clear of the security interest.

The lessor's discretion to encumber its residual interest in the goods is limited, however. §§ 2A-303, 9-407. Although creation or enforcement of a security interest in the lessor's residual interest as a general rule generally will not prejudice the lessee's rights, where enforcement of the security interest results in interference with the lessee's continuing possession and use of the goods, relief may be appropriate. § 2A-303, Official Comment 4; § 9-407. An example of this would be ownership of certain federally regulated transportation equipment by a prohibited entity, such as a foreign person.

b. Lessee's Creditors. As mentioned earlier, Article 9 further protects the lessor's residual interest against lessee grants of a security interest in the leased goods. § 9-407(b). The lessor is entitled to protect that residual interest in the goods by contractually prohibiting anyone but the lessee from possessing or using them. *Id.* See Official Comment 3. If the enforcement of a security interest granted by the lessee in its leasehold interest results in a transfer of the lessee's right to use or possess the goods, such a transfer in violation of the contractual provision triggers the lessor's remedies. The lessee could be liable to the lessor for damages caused by the transfer to the secured party to the extent that the lessor could not reasonably prevent such damage. § 2A-303(4). Also, a court may grant "other appropriate relief" to the lessor, including cancellation of the lease or an injunction against transfer.

As a general rule, a creditor (other than a holder of a mechanic's or materialman's lien) of a lessee takes subject to the lease contract (and hence of the rights of the lessor). § 2A-307(1). For instance, a secured creditor of the lessee, with a general lien on all property of the lessee, may not levy on the equipment; it must respect the lessor's rights in the goods. This parallels the requirement mentioned earlier that a creditor of the lessor must respect the leasehold interest of the lessee. § 2A-307(3).

One exception to that rule is where the lessee's creditor claims a mechanic's or materialman's lien on the goods for work done on the goods. Because the mechanic or materialman has typically preserved or enhanced the value of the goods for both the benefit of the lessee and the lessor, the mechanic's or materialman's liens will take priority "over any interest of the lessor or lessee under the lease contract or this Article" unless the statute or rule of law under which the lien arises provides otherwise. § 2A-306. So if the lessee or lessor fails to pay the mechanic responsible for repairing the equipment, both parties can lose their respective rights in the goods.

3. REALTY INTERESTS

In the event that leased goods became affixed to real estate, the rights of the lessor to the goods come into conflict with the rights of owners or mortgagees of the realty. Article 2A is remarkably helpful in resolving this conflict.

In confronting the relative claims of the lessor of any goods which, because of affixation to the real estate, have become fixtures, and of the real estate claimant who also claims the fixtures, Article 2A adopts the approach of Article 9 and subjects the lessor's interest to the filing requirements of Article 9 even though the transaction is a true lease. Thus, in most instances, the ability of the lessor to reclaim the fixtures will depend on whether or not it has, in Article 9 terms, "perfected" by giving notice. That notice is defined as the filing of a financing statement as a fixture filing. § 2A-309(1)(b), (9).

If the lessor has perfected by filing, the general rule is to favor the first in time. In effect, the lessor will have priority if three conditions are met: (i) the fixture filing is of record prior to the recorded real estate interest; (ii) the lessee has possession of the realty or an interest of record in the realty; and (iii) the lessor's interest had priority over any conflicting interest of a predecessor in title of the real estate claimant. § 2A-309(4)(b). The rule permits the lessor to prime subsequently recorded owners or encumbrancers if the lessor would have priority over any predecessor owner or encumbrancer. Such a predecessor could be the lessee itself or a prior owner who had delivered a waiver or subordination agreement.

Even if the lessor was not first in time, it will still have priority if its lease was a "purchase money lease" (meaning the lessee did not have any right to use or possess the goods prior to the lease) and the lessor perfected within ten days after the goods were affixed to the real estate. § 2A-309(4)(a). So if the lessee does not own the realty free and clear, all that a purchase money lessor has to do is file a financing statement, within ten days of when the goods are affixed to the real estate, in order to take priority over any third-party owner or encumbrancer. This is an improvement over pre-2A law in many jurisdictions, where a signed waiver was necessary.

If the lessor has not perfected, or cannot take advantage of the rules just discussed, it may still have the priority over the real estate financer in situations where giving the lessor priority in the goods and the ability to reclaim them does no harm to the real estate owner. There are four such situations enumerated:

(i) the fixtures are readily removable property (§ 2A-309 (5)(a));

(ii) the lien on the realty is "obtained by legal or equitable proceedings after the lease contract is enforceable" (§ 2A-309(5)(b));

(iii) the realty owner or encumbrancer has disclaimed an interest in the goods as fixtures or "has consented in a writing to the lease" (§ 2A-309(5)(c)); or

(iv) during any time, including a "reasonable" time thereafter, that the lessee "has a right to remove the goods as against the encumbrancer or owner" (§ 2A-309(5)(d)).

In all other situations, the priority rules governing conflicting interests in real estate will determine conflicting priorities between the lessor and any encumbrancer or owner. § 2A-309(7). As noted in Chapter 3.A, § 2A-309(5) grants priority to a lessor of "readily removable replacements of domestic appliances," under a consumer lease. So long as the lease agreement has become enforceable before the goods become fixtures, the lessor will prevail over any conflicting interest of the owner or any mortgagee of the realty, even if the lessor has not perfected its interest in the goods by a fixture filing.

4. OWNERS OF UNDERLYING GOODS

The leased goods may be small enough (such as a carburetor or air- conditioning unit for an automobile) to be attached to larger equipment in such a manner that the former become accessions and hence subject to prior claims of owners or secured parties having rights in the original property.

"Accessions" are goods that "are installed in or affixed to other goods." § 2A-310(1). The general rule is that the interest of the lessor or lessee under a lease contract entered into before the goods became accessions is prior to all interests in the whole. § 2A-310(2). This protection given to the lessor (or lessee) of accessions is subject to three exceptions. First, a buyer or lessee in the ordinary course of an interest in the whole will defeat the interest in the accession. § 2A-310(4)(b). Again, such ordinary course transferees are deserving of protection. Second, if a creditor's security interest in the whole was perfected before the lease contract of the accession was made, the creditor will have priority if it makes subsequent advances without knowledge of the lease of the accession. § 2A-319(4)(b). Among other things, these exceptions mean that both parties to the lease will want to restrict the other's ability to encumber, sell, or sublet the underlying goods. The lessee may want to conduct a search of UCC filings against the lessor to determine if there are any such preexisting liens.

Third, the interests of the lessor and lessee of the accession are subordinated to interests in the whole existing at the time the lease contract for the accession items was made (unless such prior interests have "disclaimed an interest in the [accessions] as part of the whole" or "have in a writing consented to the lease"). § 2A-310(3). By contrast, leasehold interests in the accessions have priority over "all subsequently acquired interests in the whole," if the accessions lease was "entered into at the time or after the goods became accessions." *Id.* A lessor of accessions who has priority may, on expiration of the lease or upon default, remove those goods from the whole, but must reimburse any holder (except the lessee itself) of an interest in the whole "for the cost of repair of any physical injury but not for any diminution in value of the whole" caused by removal of the accessions. § 2A-310(5). Anyone entitled to such reimbursement may refuse permission to remove until the party seeking removal gives "adequate security" for such reimbursement.

These rules are helpful. Lessors of accessions will be adequately protected if they obtain from the owner or encumbrancer of the underlying goods either written consent to the lease or a disclaimer of an interest in the goods; the former, however, may be simpler to obtain. These rules motivate the lessor and lessee to investigate the nature and intended use of the leased goods, and emphasize the desirability of entering into the lease, before the goods are delivered and installed as part of the larger whole.

BIBLIOGRAPHY

Peter A. Alces, *Surreptitious and Not-So-Surreptitious Adjustment of the UCC: An Introductory Essay*, 39 ALA. L. REV. 559 (1988).

Ronald M. Bayer, *Personal Property Leasing: Article 2A of the Uniform Commercial. Code*, 43 BUS. LAW. 1491 (1988).

Amelia H. Boss, *The History of Article 2A: A Lesson for Practitioner and Scholar Alike*, 39 ALA. L. REV. 575 (1988).

Lawrence F. Flick, Arti*cle 2A Leases*, 44 BUS. LAW. 1501 (1989).

Lawrence F. Flick, *Leases of Personal Property*, 45 BUS. LAW. 2331 (1990).

Larry T. Garvin, *The Changed (and Changing?) Uniform Commercial Code*, 26 FLA. ST. U. L. REV. 285 (1999).

Charles A. Heckman, *Article 2A of the Uniform Commercial Code: Government of the Lessor, by the Lessor, and for the Lessor*, 36 ST. LOUIS U. L.J. 309 (1991).

Edwin E. Huddleson, *Old Wine in New Bottles: UCC Article 2A Leases*, 39 ALA. L. REV. 615 (1988).

Huddleson et al., *UCC Annual Survey—Leases*, 58 BUS. LAW. 1567 (2003).

Huddleson, *Leasing is Distinctive*, 35 U.C.C. L.J. 15 (2003).

Sarah Howard Jenkins, *Application of the U.C.C. to Nonpayment Virtual Assets or Digital Art*, 11 DUQ. BUS. L. J. 245 (2009).

William H. Lawrence & John H. Minan, *The Law of Personal Property Leasing*, 34 SANTA CLARA L. REV. 1303 (1994) (book review).

Fred H. Miller, *Consumer Leases under Uniform Commercial Code Article 2A*, 39 ALA. L. REV. 957 (1988).

Fred H. Miller, *Modernizing the UCC for the Millennium, Introduction to a Collection on the New UCC*, 25 OKLA. CITY U. L. REV. 189 (2000).

Charles W. Mooney, Jr., *Personal Property Leasing: A Challenge*, 36 BUS. LAW. 1605 (1981).

Jane Derse Quasarano, *Commercial Transactions and Contracts*, 39 WAYNE L. REV. 399 (1993).

Daryl B. Robertson, *The UCC in Transition: Guardians of the Code*

Revise Commercial Law, 38 N.C. St Bus. Q. 26 (1991).

Robert H. Storm, UCC *Now Governs Personal Property Leases*, 65 Wis. L. Rev. 181 (1992).

Robert D. Strauss, *Equipment Leases under Article 2A*, 43 Mercer L. Rev. 853 (1992).

Robert D. Strauss & Lawrence F. Flick, *Leases*, 46 Bus. Law. 1509 (1991).

Symposium, *Out with the Old, In with the New? Articles 2 and 2A of the Uniform Commercial Code*, 3 DePaul Bus. & Comm. L.J. 513 (2004-2005).

Stephen T. Whelan, New York's Uniform Commercial Code New Article 2A (1994).

Stephen T. Whelan et al., *Leases*, 50 Bus. Law. 1481 (1995).

Stephen T. Whelan & Robert D. Strauss, *Leases*, 49 Bus. Law. 1857 (1994).

Stephen T. Whelan et al., *Leases*, 66 Bus. Law. 1101 (2011).

Interpretation

Richard L. Barnes, *Distinguishing Sales and Leases: A Primer on the Scope and Purpose of UCC Article 2A*, 25 U. Mem. L. Rev. 873 (1995).

Lisa L. DeCecco, *Article 2A Will Not Be Successful until Complete: Opportunity to Meet the Challenge Still Exists*, 9 J.L. & Com. 299 (1989).

Steven L. Harris, *The Rights of Creditors under Article 2A*, 39 Ala. L. Rev. 803 (1988).

Michael J. Herbert, *A Draft Too Soon: Article 2A of the Uniform Commercial Code*, 93 Com. L.J. 413 (1988).

Michael J. Herbert, *Unconscionability under Article 2A*, 21 U. Tol. L. Rev. 715 (1990).

John Levin, *Lease Terms Implied under UCC Article 2A*, 27 U.C.C. L.J. 227 (1995).

Donald J. Rapson, The Emerged and Emerging Uniform Commercial Code: Impact of Article 2A (as Amended in 1990) on Secured Transactions Under Article 9, West C812 ALI-ABA 183 (Nov. 1992).

Ian Shrank and Samuel Yim, *Liquidated Damages in Commercial Leases of Personality—the Proper Analysis*, 64 Bus. Law. 757 (2009).

Edwin E. Smith & Marijane Benner Browne, THE EMERGED AND EMERGING NEW UNIFORM COMMERCIAL CODE: UCC ARTICLE 2A INTEREST AS COLLATERAL, WEST C965 ALI-ABA 17 (Dec. 1994).

True Lease Definition

Richard L. Barnes. *Distinguishing Sales and Leases: A Primer on the Scope and Purpose of UCC Article 2A*, 25 U. MEM. L. REV. 873 (1995).

Amelia H. Boss, *True Lease or Secured Transaction: The New Definition of UCC Section 1-201(37)*, 44 CONSUMER FIN. L.Q. Rep. 3 (1990).

Corinne Cooper, *Identifying a Personal Property Lease Under the UCC*, 49 OHIO ST. L.J. 195, 203 (1988).

Laurie L. Dawley, Comment, *The Continuing Debate Regarding the Lease Versus Disguised Security Interest Issue: Did the Edison Court Correctly Find a True Lease?* 24 J. CORP. L. 169 (1998).

Daniel Hemel, *The Economic Logic of the Lease/Loan Distinction in Bankruptcy*, 120 YALE L. J. 1492 (2011).

E. Carolyn Hochstadter Dicker and John P. Campo, *FF&E and the True Lease Question: Article 2A and Accompanying Amendments to UCC Section 1-201(37)*, 7 AM. BANKR. INST. L. REV. 517 (1999).

Robert W. Ihne, *Seeking a Meaning for "Meaningful Residual Value" and the Reality of "Economic Realities"—An Alternative Roadmap for Distinguishing Trues Leases from Security Interests*, 62 Bus. LAW. 1439 (2007).

John C. Murray, *Synthetic Leases: "Bankruptcy Proofing" The Lessee's Option to Purchase*, 106 COM. L.J. 221 (2001).

H. Peter Nesvold, *What Are You Trying to Hide? Synthetic Leases, Financial Disclosure, and the Information Mosaic*, 4 STAN. J.L. Bus. & FIN. 83 (1999).

Raymond T. Nimmer, *U.C.C. Article 2A: The New Face of Leasing*, 3 DEPAUL BUS. & COMM. L.J. 559 (2004-2005).

Laura J. Paglia, *U.C.C. Article 2A Distinguishing between True Leases and Secured Sales*, 63 ST. JOHN'S L. REV. 69 (1988).

Finance Leases

Michael W. Gaines, *Security Interests under Article 2A: More Confusion in the Leasing Arena*, 18 Stetson L. Rev. 69 (1988).

Joseph W. Gelb et al., *Recent Developments in Usury Law and Personal Property Lease Recharacterization*, 45 Bus. Law. 1799 (1990).

David A. Levy, *Financial Leasing under the UNIDROIT Convention and the Uniform Commercial Code: A Comparative Analysis*, 5 Ind. Int'l & Comp. L. Rev. 267 (1995).

Stephen T. Whelan, *The Emerging Definition of a UCC 2A "Finance Lease,"* World Leasing News (July 2008).

Consumer Leases

Ralph J. Rohner, *Leasing Consumer Goods: The Spotlight Shifts to the Uniform Consumer Leases Act*, 35 Conn. L. Rev. 647, 649 (2003).

Irma S. Russell, *Got Wheels? Article 2A, Standardized Rental Car Terms, Rational Inaction, and Unilateral Private Ordering*, 40 Loy L.A. L. Rev. 137, 138 (2006).

ABOUT THE AUTHORS

Amelia H. Boss, a graduate of Bryn Mawr College and Rutgers Camden Law School, is the Trustee Professor of Law at Drexel University's Earle Mack School of Law, where she teaches in the commercial law, bankruptcy, and electronic commerce areas. She is a member of the Permanent Editorial Board of the Uniform Commercial Code, the former chair of the Uniform Commercial Code Committee of the American Bar Association, and a former chair of the Business Law Section of the American Bar Association. She also serves on the governing Council of the American Law Institute.

Professor Boss served as the American Law Institute member of the drafting committees to revise UCC Article 2 (sales), Article 2A (leases) Article 2B (licensing of software), and Article 1 (general provisions). In the past, she served as an advisor/observer to the revisions on Article 5 (letters of credit) and Article 8 (investment securities). She also served on the ALI's members' consultative group on the RESTATEMENT OF THE LAW OF SURETYSHIP, and as the American Bar Association Advisor to the Uniform Electronic Transactions Act. Professor Boss is a member of the American Bar Foundation, a fellow and member of the Board of Regents of the American College of Commercial Finance Lawyers, and a member of the board of directors of the Institute of International Commercial Law. She has served as an advisor and as the U.S. delegate to the United Nations Commission on International Trade Law (UNCITRAL) on issues relating to electronic commerce. She has written extensively in the areas of commercial law and electronic commerce.

Stephen T. Whelan is a partner in the New York office of law firm Blank Rome LLP, where he specializes in lease financings, secured lending, asset securitization and energy finance. Mr. Whelan is a graduate of Princeton University and Harvard Law School, and is former chair of the subcommittee on leasing of the Uniform Commercial Code Committee in the American Bar Association's Section of Business Law. He is a member of the American Law Institute, a Visiting Lecturer on constitutional law at Princeton University, and a member of the board of directors of the Equipment Leasing and Finance Association. Mr. Whelan is co-author of the ABA Annual Survey on Leases, author of the securitization chapters in the Matthew Bender & Co. treatises on Equipment Leasing and Commercial Finance, and author of three other books on UCC 2A. He is chairman of the trustees of the Witherspoon Institute (Princeton, NJ); an advisory counsel member of the James Madison Program at Princeton University; a Fellow of The American College of Commercial Finance Lawyers; and a Fellow of The American College of Investment Counsel.